Abby & GG Get Going

A 21st Century Grand Tour

by
April Gamble

the Peppertree Press
Sarasota, Florida

Copyright © April Gamble, 2014

All rights reserved. Published by the Peppertree Press, LLC. the Peppertree Press and associated logos are trademarks of the Peppertree Press, LLC.

No part of this publication may be reproduced, stored in a retrieval system, transmitted in any form or by any means, electronic, mechanical, photocopying, recording, or otherwise, without prior written permission of the publisher and author/illustrator.
Graphic design by Rebecca Barbier.
Photos by Jeff Caroll.

For information regarding permission,
call 941-922-2662 or contact us at our website:
www.peppertreepublishing.com or write to:
the Peppertree Press, LLC.
Attention: Publisher
1269 First Street, Suite 7
Sarasota, Florida 34236

ISBN: 978-1-61493-250-5

Library of Congress Number: 2014904095

Printed in the U.S.A.

Printed April 2014

*Dedicated to
Abby Carroll*

With Thanks

To Jeff Carroll, a terrific son who always has my back, to Abigail and Penelope Carroll, for all the joy, and to their friends who allowed me to use their names in the stories, which made writing them so much fun.

This book is entirely a work of fiction.
Making it all up was a blast.

Itinerary

Prologue - - - - - - - - - - - - - - - - 7

London, England - - - - - - - - - - - 11
Florence, Italy - - - - - - - - - - - - - 71
Rome, Italy - - - - - - - - - - - - - - 149
Paris, France - - - - - - - - - - - - - - 163

Helpful Information - - - - - - - - 215
About the Author - - - - - - - - - - 219

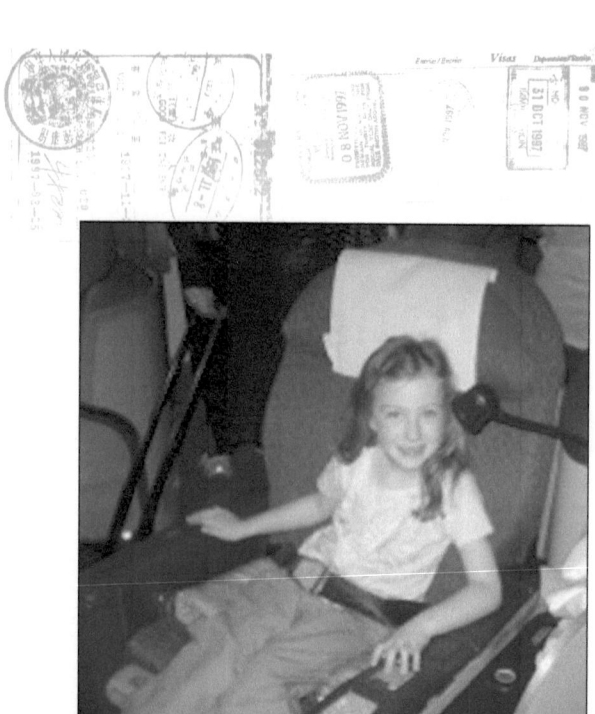

PROLOGUE

I LOVE MY DAD AND I LOVE MY MOM. They are divorced and that stinks. I have a little sister Penny. She is so cute. She has reddish-blond hair, and sometimes I call her lollypop because she looks like a cherry lollypop to me. She is skinny on the bottom and a puffy swirl of pink on top. Penny is six years younger than I am. She's a chatterbox and can always make me laugh.

We are always going back and forth between our parents' houses. Sometimes it feels like we are always moving, always packing up and on the go. My parents feel bad about it, but right now my life is just a lot of back and forth. It could make a kid seasick. The secret is, I have grown so used to moving around that there is nothing I like more than packing up, getting on a plane, and going somewhere.

That is where my grandmother GG comes in. We travel a great deal in our family, but once a year just the two of us go off to a new big city. GG calls it a 21st Century Grand Tour. She told me a hundred years ago young ladies were taken to the major cities in Europe to learn about art and history and culture, and that is our plan too.

I live in California and GG lives on Fisher Island, which is a real island you get to on a boat. She also lives in London, England, where we usually meet up. England is where the Queen lives. My Dad says GG thinks she is the real Queen.

My grandfather Ted died a long time ago, so GG has oodles of time to plan our trips, and she plans ever detail. Every single detail, but sometimes those careful plans collapse, just plop. GG says our motto is the F-word. Flexibility. And when our plans go kaput, out comes Plan B, which she makes up on the spot.

GG also has dozens of maps and guidebooks, which she always wants to show me. I asked her once if she knew all that information was available nice and easy on the Internet and she said sure she did, but she just likes to do some things the old-fashioned way. Which I guess is what grandmothers like to do.

With GG good manners are a must, and she has all kinds of rules and wacky ideas. Hearing all this you might think she would be hard to get along with and no fun at all on our special trips, but somehow she is the opposite. We laugh all the time. GG likes to be silly, and she really likes me.

GG is addicted to fancy, tall shoes. She cannot pass a shoe store without going inside. The shoes always hurt her feet, and she hobbles around pretending the shoes don't hurt, like I can't tell. I never let her get away with that one.

GG is my Dad's Mom. Since the divorce, GG doesn't seem to like my Mom. If she even says her name she gets a funny look on her face like she ate something yucky. But she never says anything bad about my Mom. Never. GG said she would always be nice to my Mom to insure she will get the permission for our special trips together, and she will do whatever it takes. I am glad she does, because I really look forward to our trips and I have learned a lot. I have been to the most amazing places that none of my friends have seen. And don't be fooled into thinking these are dull visits to museums and towns to look at old bits of wood and rocks, because we don't just see things; we do things.

We have been on the tops of tall buildings, hunted by villains, cold and scared, eaten weird food, stayed in palaces, taken helicopters rides, gone to grand parties, met celebrities, and spent a zillion dollars on shoes. Once in a panic to save her from an attacker I gave the man a black eye and tore his nose with a Barbie. GG just has a way of tumbling into trouble; anything can happen when we are together. Have you ever been arrested? I have, well almost. Misunderstandings are what she calls them, and that can mean big trouble.

Well now that you have met us it is time to get going.

Wheels up.

London, England

"Are you all set, Cupcake"?

"Passport, IPad, and gummy bears, all ready." I gave my Dad a playful salute.

My little sister loves stuffed toys, so when Penny handed over her favorite stuffed bear to take along I considered that a very generous departure gift. My backpack was already pretty full, but I set it on the floor and stuffed the teddy inside, then gave my sister a big kiss.

"Thank you, Lollypop, I am going to miss you." GG once told me she liked the fact that there was six years' difference in the ages of her granddaughters. She would be able to travel alone with me for a number of years, and when I am a teenager and probably more interested in spending my free time with my friends, she could then begin travelling with Penny to all of the places she had shown me. To GG this idea provided many years of happy travel anticipation. The problem with that theory is I cannot imagine not wanting to take trips with her, and I also know if in the future I want to bring a friend along she will probably say yes.

Today I was at LAX. The first thing I have to do when I leave California is get on a huge plane. It holds about 350 people. My Dad usually drives me to Los Angeles because he insists on no plane changes. I am glad, because that would be kind of scary.

"Have a great time with your grandmother, but remember not to get dragged into any of her ..."

"Misunderstandings, Dad?"

"Yeah, Cupcake, those," he said with slight sarcasm.

My Dad had told me he knew from firsthand experience world travel is very useful in showing, not just telling, what makes other people and cultures different, but more importantly what makes them the same. He was pleased with my grandmother's good intentions, but less so at some of the outcomes.

GG was always optimistic and often told me she was proud of her tutelage provided by our travels and we should not allow the occasional misunderstanding that had cropped up along the way to dampen our enthusiasm. Works for me.

I have already been to many places, but the Grand Tour was just GG and I. Today we were headed to Switzerland.

GG had wanted to take me to Cairo, Egypt, to see the pyramids and that sounded amazing, but my parents said at this time it was not safe. So instead, GG decided on Switzerland, which she felt the lakes and the Matterhorn would be a huge contrast to big cities and the small coastal town of Santa Barbara. I was excited to see what this new place had to offer. The only Matterhorn I had ever seen was at Disneyland.

I gave my Dad another big goodbye kiss. When I said goodbye again to Penny she started to cry.

"No, Abby, don't go away. I want you to stay with me and Daddy." Now she was even louder. My Dad picked her up and gave her a cuddle and a big wink to me.

"Daddy, can I have a Hello Kitty book?" was the last thing I heard as I walked with my escort through the security door.

The plane ride is long and boring, and I usually just watch DVDs and eat ice cream until I get sleepy. I get to fly first class because GG has loads of frequent flyer miles. I think she gets them from buying all those shoes.

After just about forever I arrived at my first stop: Heathrow Airport in London, England. This is where GG and I meet up.

This place is gigantic and noisy. As I made my way up the long ramp, a lady with a huge purse ran her wheelie bag right over my foot. "Ouch" just popped out of my mouth. I looked right at her, expecting her to say excuse me or sorry, but she didn't say anything. Then she scowled at me as if I owed her an apology.

I wanted to say "Hey lady, I am just a kid, but I know when someone is being rude." But I didn't say anything and just kept walking.

You have to walk and walk and walk to get out of the building, which I don't mind after I have been sitting on a plane for eleven and a half hours. That is right, eleven-plus long hours. That is like two full school days in a row with no recess.

I have been at this airport before, but it is always a confusing place so I am really glad there is an airline escort to help me.

Passport Control is my first stop and is where each country

identifies who is coming into their country and where they are coming from. Sometimes the lines are very long, but it is a rather interesting place. It is usually eerily quiet because everyone is tired from his or her long journey. It smells pretty funky in there too.

There are people from all over the world. I love looking at all of the different clothes and styles. There are dark African women in vivid colors with huge scarves wrapped around their heads. They look beautiful. I wish I could ask them how they get the scarves to stand up so high.

The ladies from India are in bright colors with red and gold and silver. Their dresses wrap around and around them with long pieces of cloth. Some even really old ladies show their tummies, and that makes me giggle. Some of the Indian men and even boys wear turbans on their heads and they never cut their hair, just keep it tucked in their hats. I often wonder if they sleep in those hats, but I have never had anyone to ask.

Some Arab ladies wear long dresses that look like black nightgowns. Many of them wear black veils and masks on their faces so all you can see are their dark eyes. They are very mysterious. Some Arab men wear long dresses of the whitest white and sheets on their heads. I think they look like elegant salt and pepper standing there.

I also saw some men and boys with black suits and flat black hats and long curls hanging down the side of their faces. These are normal clothes for them, and they probably think I look peculiar in my jeans and sweater.

"Thank you," I said to the agent when he stamped my passport. I was officially in England now.

Pushing through the large clattering metal doors to the welcome hall of Terminal One, I looked around and did not see GG, who was usually making noise and waving wildly.

Just then she burst through the waiting crowd, her elbows busy clearing a path. "Here I am!" She was calling out to me while jumping up and down like a monkey in a banana store. Sometimes it is embarrassing she is so loud, but it does help me find her.

She grabbed me in a big hug, then quickly signed the release offered by the escort.

"And just how is my favorite traveling companion?" She didn't let me reply. "Look at you. You are prettier and even taller."

"I'm a kid, GG, we grow, it is kind of our job." As most kids, that tiresome old line about growing every time we are greeted by an adult is a bit boring. Usually GG was not so dull, but I had bought all new clothes for this trip and GG was right that I had grown a little more than usual.

"Abby, we probably should have just stayed at an airport hotel tonight as our flight out is very early, but I know you want to see the flat and besides I did not finish my packing yet." We chattered nonstop as we waited in the taxi queue huddled under the shelter, for as usual it was raining in London. "I hope you are hungry? Rose is making those little sandwiches you like."

Rose is my grandmother's housekeeper. She has worked for GG for more than 25 years. During that time a lot had happened. GG told me they are best friends, and both relied on the other to make their lives better. I have known Rose my whole life. I like her.

"My darling girl, come and give me another hug." GG always calls me names like darling girl, sweetheart, sweetie, and a bunch of others. Sometimes GG calls my Dad Wheels. So do some of his friends. GG told me that when he was a little boy he never went anywhere without a toy car in his pocket. At night he surrounded his bed with giant yellow Tonka trucks. He has always loved anything with wheels. He went crazy for his bicycle and even begged her to let him keep it in his bedroom. Then motorcycles and cars, so everyone just started calling him Wheels. Sometimes I call him Wheels, and it always makes him laugh. Cupcake, Wheels, and Lollypop; what a family.

Riding in the taxi to Westminster, we were heading to GG's big condo on the Thames River, right in the middle of London. Queen Elizabeth owns the property the building sits on. She owns most of London and what she doesn't own is owned by her cousin the Duke of Westminster. They are mega rich, which I guess is how she paid for her crown with all the big diamonds and rubies.

GG turned to me and winked. "How is Wheels doing?"

"Life is good, that's what he says." We continued in our lively conversation. Then all of the sudden GG gasped, "The stewardess told you what?"

I sat up straight and looked into GG's face. "She told me the strike begins at midnight tonight."

"Strike!" GG shrieked as she threw her hands up. "Those overpaid flying waiters are going on strike! This is a disaster. Our visit to Switzerland may be in jeopardy."

"The cabin attendant is a waiter?" I asked. "Oh, you mean because she gives us our dinner? One showed us how to put on our life jackets, and a real nice man found me an extra pillow for my American Girl doll."

"Yes, yes, they do a lot of things when they actually show up, but a strike means they do nothing at all." She sounded slightly annoyed that I was defending the militant cabin crew.

"I will get online as soon as we are back to the house and see just what is going on." Her only concern was how to salvage our journey to Switzerland.

Before she departed for the day, Rose had laid out a yummy spread of cakes and sandwiches, and the flat felt warm and welcoming when we arrived. I went right to the cookies.

GG went straight to her office. The room was the smallest in her house, but really nice, with built-in desk and cupboards in dark wood and on the main wall opposite the window was a large world map. The map had blue electronic pushpins highlighting all the places we had visited. And red pins in the cities that GG planned for us to visit in the future. GG sat at her computer.

The computer was one of the slickest high-end models sold for personal use. My Dad had been shocked when she bought it, because she doesn't even like to use her cell phone.

But today she was clicking away in full command. First she found the local news.

"Abby, you were right, a strike has been called." The three-day strike action was indeed on, and most planes were grounded for the next 72 hours. GG quickly went next to the airline site to see if they had suggestions or information. They did, but nothing actually useful to us. The airlines would try to operate their long-haul flights of over six hours with substitute cabin attendants, but their shorter flights would be sacrificed.

Thoroughly disgusted, but with no time to fume, GG was not to be thwarted. "We shall take the Orient Express train; it goes right through the Alps. Just let me figure out how to book all of this." GG prided herself in her travel-planning skills that the Internet had made so easy and went right to work checking availability. GG said all of this out loud though I was in the other room and could not hear her.

GG is a doer. If she doesn't like something or if a plan doesn't work out, she doesn't just pout or grumble, she fixes the problem, usually right away. I try to do that too. It is not always easy to do, and today's dilemma seemed to have her vexed.

"Phooey, it says that they are fully booked for the next two days. I should think in an emergency they could attach another train car or two." GG was still talking to an empty room, but just about then I stuck my head in the door.

"How ya doing in here? Are we going, or what?" I was nibbling a strawberry.

"Sweetie, we will not give up. I think I will call a friend of mine who just may be able to help." I handed her a cold Pepsi.

GG's friend had already left his office. "Please, this is an emergency," she explained our predicament to his secretary and requested he return her call. She took a big gulp, then stood up and ushered me from the office.

"Abby, I am not optimistic about our chances of getting on that train, but if it is at all possible, Colonel Marmaduke Pickle will come to our rescue. He is a big shot at the Orient Express."

I abruptly stopped and turned my head to look up at her. "GG, no one is really named Marmaduke Pickle; you are making that up?"

"No, I promise I'm not. He is an ever so dignified gentleman." I giggled a bit.

"I am sorry to say and it seems unfair, but his name makes me laugh too."

"GG, what is your real name? You told me the GG was for Grandmother Gable, but everyone calls you GG?"

She winked. "It's a secret I will tell you someday." Then with a loud throat clearing meant to change the subject she said, "His wife Bunny is one of my best friends."

"Her name is Bunny Pickle?" I asked, disbelieving and again certain my grandmother's colorful conversation and imagination had made up these names.

"Well, her real name is Beatrice, but we have always called her Bunny. You know the British upper class love peculiar monikers. All very PG Wodehouse."

"Who?"

"Wodehouse. He is a marvelous British author. I don't suppose you have read him yet, but you will. He is a treat."

Just then the phone rang and GG grabbed it in the entry

hall. It was the gherkin. All of this talk about pickles made me hungry. I went back to the food and grabbed a sandwich.

"Hullo, GG," greeted Duke, as his friends knew him.

"Duke, we are desperate to get to Switzerland. Can you find us a cabin?"

"Sorry to disappoint you, but the train is fully booked for the next three days.

"Oh no. What about extra cars?" GG pleaded, practically stamping her foot.

"It's this blasted global economy. A Chinese Trade Commission has booked it all, including the maximum extra cars. You may just have to have your adventure closer to home."

GG thanked him and then hung up the phone with a feeling of great discouragement. This certainly was not a normal feeling for GG. She was usually rather dogged and managed to get what she wanted at least most of the time, but this was not looking promising. If she booked our trip for three days from now it would take another day to get there, and the week would just about be over. Not nearly enough time to satisfy our itinerary.

GG went to the dining room to find me and to admit defeat. There in the sunny window facing the river Thames I sat nibbling on my sandwich. GG did not have a chance to begin when I said, "Sometime I wish you would plan for us to stay in London for our week together. There is so much to see and do here. I know I have seen a great deal, but that was when I was little and I don't really remember much of it. Now all I ever get to see is the road to and from Heathrow and sometimes a quick stop at Harrods."

GG brightened. "That is my surprise! We are actually going to stay right here all week, and I am going to show you all of the treasures of this wonderful city. And why I think right here is the center of the world." GG beamed with pride in her city and also with having a Plan B so easily. For GG it is always essential to have a Plan B when travelling. "Remember, our family motto is, Flexibility. Now please share those lovely salmon sandwiches."

The next morning when I emerged from my bedroom I found GG with maps and guide books spread all over the dining room. GG glanced up. "Good morning, sweetie. Grab a muffin and come look. First we must plan our assault on the city." GG loves maps and travel planning, and it showed on her face. Routes, details, and time lines were never left to chance. I am a little more spontaneous than that, but GG assured me with a game plan you get a lot more done.

I picked up a pastry from a silver basket and circled the table. GG looked up again from her map with a double take. Her face fell. "Why, may I ask, are you wearing that?" I had emerged in a fringed chamois skirt and red gingham blouse. I was wearing cowboy boots.

I am used to GG's first reaction to my clothes always being a bit skeptical. She loves to dress fancy, but me, I am more Boho Chic, but for our trips she always has a theme. Looking me over, GG tightened her lips, then raised her eyebrows high and they started to dance. Right after that agonizing performance she offered me a bit of unsolicited advice.

Well, sweetie, maybe not exactly right for this trip." My Dad says GG offers advice on just about everything like it is her job to be bossy. It drives him nuts, but he told me the trick is to nod your head and smile at her. So that's what I did. Smile and nod and soon she will forget all about it, probably, because her feet hurt so much.

Here we go again I thought, as I stood tall. Smile and nod. "I used the money you sent to buy traveling togs; you picked the theme."

Oh yeah, have you ever in your life heard another person say togs when they mean clothes? Nope, me neither, but GG does, she says things like that all the time.

"My theme?"

"It was a little bit confusing at first, but Kora told me equine means horse, so Mom took me to the Western store."

"Horse?" Then suddenly GG jolted upright. "Oh no! Not equine, alpine. Darling, I said the theme was alpine. For Switzerland get alpine clothes. What have you done?"

GG was almost too stunned to speak. She swallowed deeply. "Honey, that Hee Haw attire might be a bit flashy. Let's try something a little more discreet. Ok?"

"Ok, discreet it shall be. Do I need to get a bowling hat or something?"

"You mean a bowler. No, they are for prissy bankers and lodge attendants, all men. No, what you need is a trip to Harrods."

I groaned. "Please don't take me to Harrods. That is the only place in London I ever go. Can't we go somewhere else?" I grabbed another pastry and took a big bite.

This request annoyed GG. Harrods is her favorite, but I was determined not to go all the way to Europe just to go shopping. I don't like shopping. To me it's boring to wander around inside a store, and Harrods was so big I knew it would take hours. GG always bought everything in the place, and I would end up with a pile of things I don't really want. And worse, I would probably have to wear some of the things. I licked the glaze off my bear claw and then took a drink of milk.

"Yes, of course. There are many trendy places to shop. I can be young and cool too, just look at those photos on the piano. Now don't I look positively fantastic?" GG was beaming.

"You look skinny. How old is this picture?"

GG ignored the age part. "Just look how pretty I am in the photo with your Grandfather Ted."

"You do look pretty, and he is very handsome too." I know that my grandmother is really mushy over Grandpa Ted, and just saying his name made her happy. Big smile.

"We have loads of choices here in London, but touring first and shopping later." GG was stirring her coffee and examining the goodies in the basket.

"Sounds right to me. Where to?"

"The Tower of London." GG's head popped up. "It is a huge, ancient palace fortress, and the tower was the prison. They have a great tour, and we will learn all about the place." Her voice made it sound very important.

"I don't know if you remember, but about six years ago your Dad and I took you. Actually, you fell asleep in your stroller before we arrived and never woke up until the taxi ride back to the flat."

"I don't remember it at all."

"It is a must see. You may have read about it in school. It is where King Henry the 8th lived and where I believe several of his wives were beheaded," GG said playfully as she ran a finger across her throat in a slicing motion. She then took a lick of the raspberry jam, which had oozed onto her fingers.

"Ick," I said as she nibbled on a strawberry. "Chopping off heads sounds gross. Do we have to see that?"

"Positively barbaric." Leaving the gruesome conversation behind, GG perked up. "They keep the Crown Jewels there, and we girls can never see too many sparklers, right?"

I had been to many jewelry stores with my grandmother; she is well known for her bling.

While GG quickly showered and changed into a well-tailored, soft rose-colored pantsuit and dangerously high new hot-pink suede pumps, I changed too.

When I entered the room in yet another of my equine wardrobe, GG said nothing. She was unable to speak. She just nudged me toward the door. For the record, I liked my outfit.

The Tower of London is huge and menacing, just as GG had described. We started with the public Beefeaters Tour, and learned all the historical dates and events. History is one of my favorite classes, so this place was really interesting to me.

After the tour we wandered through the Crown Jewel House. Wow. I soon joined the chorus of ohs and ahs as we gawking visitors slowly passed the heavy dark glass cases displaying the magnificent state pieces. There were jewel-encrusted crowns, scepters, sashes, and goblets, some which are still in use at special British Royal occasions.

Bright and sunny, it was such a lovely day that we agreed we should take full advantage of the good weather and take a boat ride back to Westminster. Naturally, after a stop at the gift shop for souvenirs. We exited the Palace and headed to the docks nearby. We held hands and were swinging them back and forth as we were skipping along. Actually, I skipped, but GG's feet were protesting after all the stone stairs at the Tower so she was more accurately shuffling. I didn't actually feel she deserved sore feet, but she knows what causes it and refuses to fix the problem.

Waiting in line for tickets to board the Thames boat, we were still gabbing about the jewels we had just seen when we observed a young downtrodden woman standing a few places ahead of us in the line. She was pregnant and already had two small children. One child was asleep, but the other was busy kicking the stroller and wiping her nose on the tail of her mother's shabby coat. The woman was inquiring about the cost of the journey. We did not hear what she was told, but the woman shook her head, then turned and left the queue without tickets.

When it was our turn, GG purchased the tickets and when she left the ticket line she looked around. I thought she might be looking for the lady so I pointed to the woman, who now stood near a snack bar. She was fussing with her baby stroller and trying to calm the crying toddler. GG took my arm and went up to the mother and thrust tickets for the boat and a wad of cash into the hands of the astonished woman. Without a word GG turned us around and quickly pulled me on board our boat.

"GG, why did you buy tickets for that lady you don't know?"

"Oh sweetie, she forgot her handbag and she told me she would send me the money later." But I had seen the lady's purse hanging on her arm. The woman had said nothing at all to GG. She didn't have time.

I know my Grandmother was just being generous. She did things like this all the time and never talked about it. I wondered why GG didn't want anyone to know. One time I asked her and she told me generosity will make everyone feel good, the one that gives and the one that receives.

The Thames River is the most important river in England. It is long and twisty and has very high tides that move the tea-brown water back and forth twice a day. The river isn't dirty, just muddy from the strong currents, which are dangerous and over the centuries have had many sinister tales to tell.

Boarding the barge-style vessel GG was thrilled to get the best seats on the front of the boat. Of course, there had been a few contenders, but none with the determination that GG had shown as she pushed us to the front of the crowd.

GG patted the space beside her with triumph in her voice. "Come, sweetie, have a seat."

I wiggled into the space. We had been walking for a long time, so I found the plastic seat pretty comfy.

"Dear, please pass me the sunscreen from our tote bag. Oh, and the camera too." I gave her the camera, but kept the tube of sunscreen and thought I would apply some first.

It was an idyllic day for a boat ride. The sun was bright

and the boat drifted slowly along the curvy path north while the captain pointed out many places of interest along the way, with corny banter, no doubt with hopes of increasing the disembarkation gratuities.

Leaning on the rail just behind me was a pretty lady that GG kept eyeing. The woman kept looking around at us and then again at the water. Her facial expression was tight and serious. GG shifted in her chair to look at the woman again.

I was looking at GG, as the woman was right behind me my view of her was not great. All at once, the woman slyly pulled something from inside her jacket and slid it smoothly over the side.GG sputtered, "Gun," and as she had been taking photos right along quickly tilted her camera in an attempt to click off a photo of the woman's mysterious actions. The woman saw GG's attempt and jutted forward, bumping GG's arm, causing the little camera to fly overboard.

"Oh no. What do you think you are doing?" GG was on her feet in a jump. "That was intentional." Now I was turned around and looking directly at the woman.

"Look what you have done!" I said.

GG roared. "That camera is new and was full of our holiday photos. I am reporting you." GG was furious, but the woman did not react. It almost looked like she was smirking at us.

My eyes locked on GG, saucers of astonishment at my grandmother's outburst and of the woman's mysterious behavior. When GG gets cross she says her hair is on fire. I have seen her pretty mad, but I have never seen that actually happen. I could tell she was cross because her face was purple and her eyes were in a tight, furious squint. I thought if her hair were ever going to blaze, it would right about now.

Two old women sitting nearby were now glaring in our direction. When GG stomped off to find the attendant, I was certain she would not be able to use them as witnesses.

"Captain, that woman in the front just threw my camera in the water. And she also threw a gun in the water. You need to restrain her or something before she throws in a child or heaven knows what!"

"Slow down, lady," said the attendant. His voice, deep and raspy, seemed not to have been used in a while. "Have you been hurt? If you have, we have to fill out an incident report." He handed GG a stubby pencil and small card with a tea stain ring in the middle. GG refused the items with a shake of her head. "And you say you dropped your camera. Well, you see the sign," he said while raising his beefy arm and pointing to a small printed notice on the wall. "We are not responsible for lost or damaged property," explained the unsympathetic crewmember.

"No, I am not hurt, and I did not drop my camera." GG's approach was not engendering sympathy. And the crewman seemed ready to end their chat. "That woman threw it in the river." But as GG turned to again point out the woman, she was nowhere to be seen. I had grabbed our bag and joined GG.

The two old ladies were now comfortably seated on our chairs in the front row. "You are useless," GG shouted to the florid-faced man. With a huff she took my hand, "Come on, sweetie, let's go below to the snack bar and get some refreshments."

As the boat docked and the disembarkation announcements were made, GG scrambled to get her shoes on, which she had kicked off while we had our snack. GG told me her plan was to apprehend the woman on the gangway. "I will let you know if I see her, GG, but it's pretty crowded and maybe I am too short?" I crumpled my empty potato chip bag and tossed it in the nearby bin. GG then took a last sip and handed me her lemonade bottle and I trashed that as well. I reached in the tote and grabbed two wet wipes, offering one to GG.

"Exactly why I wear tall shoes." She cleaned her hands, then jutted her chin and smiled at me as if proving the shoes were a practical issue and not her vanity. However, the plan did not work, as GG was too slow getting her now-swollen feet back into her shoes and then getting us up the steps from the snack bar. The woman had vanished.

"Don't you think that was suspicious behavior?"

"It does seem like she was hiding."

"Come on, kiddo, I think as good citizens we need to report her".

"I thought you already did?" I replied, knowing my grandmother was not one to give up.

"A total ignoramus. That floating buffoon did not want to hear anything that was going to cause him paperwork. I think this is a matter for Scotland Yard."

"Scotland?" We were pushing through the crowd.

"No, it is right here. Scotland Yard is what they call the main police station in London. And it is nearby too."

Onto the crowded, heaving dock we slowly made our way to the street and scrambled up and over the curb to flag down a taxi. "Keep an eye out for her, Abby," she instructed me as she slowly turned full circle.

"Take us to Scotland Yard, please," GG ordered the driver as we climbed into the back of a black taxi.

"You know it is only across the square there," the driver said pointing. "Are you sure you want to pay for a taxi?" he asked gently, trying to discourage us.

"Yes I do, young man, we have urgent business, so please get on it." Normally, GG would have been more than happy to walk the short distance, but now her feet were clearly hurting. Busted!

"GG, your feet are hurting, aren't they?"

"Just a little."

"I thought we made a deal that you are not going to wear shoes that hurt?"

"Yes, we did make a deal, but this morning these shoes did not hurt my feet and as they are new I did not know that they would. So I kept my deal." I just gave her a suspicious look, and she winked at me in reply.

Scotland Yard was the Metropolitan police and housed in a massive grey stone and marble building. It looked impossible to get out or in. We made our way to what we thought was the front entrance and were directed to yet another door, then on through a menacing security contraption. "GG, are they trying to keep the bad guys in or us out?"

"Both, I think," she laughed. "It certainly is secure."

Once inside the cavernous building, I was amazed by the size and the amount of activity. We approached the public information desk and were directed to six windows on the far wall. I tried to figure out which had the shortest line, but it seemed they all were about the same and all moving slowly. This was boring.

At first, GG waited patiently in line, but she looked at her watch constantly. When 15 minutes had gone she leaned down to me and said, "Time to get this party started." She stood tall and declared in a raised voice, "Excuse me, I would like to report a crime."

"Yes, Madame, you are in the correct line," answered the uniformed man, who went back to speaking with an elderly man at the front of the line.

Another few minutes, when the line had failed to advance, GG glanced at me, then said loudly, "Excuse me, is this where one reports a murder?" I was shocked.

Everyone froze in place and all conversation stopped.

"Please come forward, Madame," said the man at the desk waving to us. GG then strode purposefully to the front of the line with me at her heels, passing others who were still silent from her mere mention of such a ghastly crime.

"Ma'am, your name, please."

"I am GG Gable, and I would like to report a crime."

"You said something about murder? I will buzz you into the door marked no entrance." He pointed to a large grey door flanked by two well-armed policemen. "Please go through." Bzzzzzzzzzzzzzz. Clank, click, and the door latch opened and the two officers stood aside.

"Come on, honey," said GG with ever more determination.

A small tubby man greeted us. "I am sorry, ma'am, but your daughter is not allowed. She will need to wait on this bench."

"Don't be absurd. She is most certainly not waiting out here. This place is full of villains."

He ignored our protest. "How old are you, miss?" he asked while looking directly at me.

"I am nine," I responded honestly. I have been taught the police were your friends and to respect their authority.

"-teen. Nineteen, her last birthday," insisted GG as she spoke over me, undeterred by his position. "Quite short for her age." I was horrified by what she was saying. "She is coming with me." GG awkwardly pushed through the door past the now gaping man.

He then showed us to a small grey room with two chairs and a table. There were a stack of forms and one nubby pencil, and the man directed GG to fill out the top two pages, then he exited the room.

"Oh, Abby, I simply couldn't leave you alone out there. What a dreary place this is." GG glanced around, then began scribbling on the forms.

"Thanks, GG, I didn't want to stay out there by myself, but don't you think 19 is pushing it?" She ignored my question.

"I think they have put us in a room where they usually put the bad guys. Don't touch anything and please get some wet-wipes from our tote bag."

The room looked clean, but I dug in the tote and found a packet. "I will insist we be moved to better surroundings." Then, as GG took her spray perfume from her purse and begin to spritz the stale air in the room, the door banged open.

In walked a tall man with long, messy brown hair and serious dark eyes. He introduced himself as Detective Inspector Dixon.

I didn't think that in his grey suit he looked like a policeman, but thought maybe things were different in England.

He did not spend much time on chitchat and got right to it. "Mrs. Gable, I would like you to tell me right from the beginning what you have seen and heard and what has lead you to believe there has been a murder. And I would ask if perhaps your daughter should be spared this conversation?"

GG softly said, "She stays." He did not spend any further time on my presence and GG did not tell him I was her granddaughter. I sat silently with my hands folded in my lap.

After a long and detailed telling of the incident on the boat, GG sighed and sat back in her chair. She had by then forgotten she was going to demand a nicer room for the interview.

I was relaxing a bit now and started to slowly swing my legs. "I appreciate that you believe you saw a gun, but you also say it was all very fast. Is it possible that you saw another small object, perhaps a cell phone or IPod?"

"Don't be absurd. I can assure you, DI Dixon, that I am not some gadfly with nothing better to do than pester the police; besides, I know what I saw."

"Yes, it certainly does sound like you are clear on what you believe you saw." GG, always anxious to extort or hear a compliment, took this as one and sat high in her chair, her chin jutting forward in satisfaction.

"Abby, let me ask you, did you see the gun?"

I shifted in my seat and sat up straight for my interrogation. "No, sir, I didn't see a gun, I just heard a splash. It could have been our camera."

"What camera?" asked the now slightly bewildered detective.

"Our camera. It fell in the water," I answered.

"It was thrown in the water by the killer," insisted GG as she waved her arm in a flinging gesture. She was pushing it.

"Back to the gun please, Abby. Did you ever at any time see a gun or any small object in the woman's hand?"

"A gun" insisted GG.

"Please, Mrs. Gable, I must insist you quit interrupting. Please go on, Abby."

"No sir, I did not see any small things." My legs had stopped swinging and I was again stiff and still.

"Detective Dixon, Abby has gotten rather confused, and after all she is only nine."

"I thought I was 19?" I said.

This exchange confused Dixon, and he turned to GG and asked, "And how old are you, Mrs. Gable? You left it blank on the paperwork you filled out."

GG leaned forward and flattened her hands as if she were about to place them on the metal desk, but ever conscious of germs she did not. Instead, attempting to change the subject she inhaled and fixed a look of wry contempt on her face and answered sarcastically, "While you are asking me more silly questions, there is a murderer running around your city. I don't suppose you have anyone with bullet holes?"

Dixon was uncowed by GG's aggression and looked up from the paperwork. He went on smiling at her for a moment without saying anything else. Then he lightly tapped his fingers on the edge of his clipboard and he asked again, "And your age would be?"

"I am 45, there, satisfied?"

At which time an audible gasp emanated from me. I slapped my hand over my mouth, hoping to stop further emissions and stared at GG in blank astonishment. She's losing it, I thought. I was beginning to worry about my grandmother. My heart started to beat fast, and I hoped they could not hear it thump.

"Not entirely satisfied, Mrs. Gable. Now, if we could get back to the boat? Assuming you are correct about seeing a gun, why do you believe it was involved in a murder?" Dixon asked.

"That should be fairly obvious; why else would she be throwing it away? It did not slip and fall, it was deliberate."

"Do you think you would be able to tell us approximately where on the river the item…?"

"The gun," insisted GG.

"The gun," conceded the DI, "was dropped overboard?"

"Let me think, it was after the Tate Modern, and after the Oxo Tower, but before the Eye, but not under the Waterloo Bridge, because there was no shade over us. I had just turned to snap a photo of the Savoy Hotel. It had been where my late husband Ted and I first stayed in London, and it was just about exactly there." She was babbling. "Is that helpful?"

"Yes, very thorough," said the DI as he continued to make notes.

"Are you going to get the gun?" I asked.

"Yes, are you going to send divers down?" said GG.

"Probably not today. Do you think you could identify the woman again if you saw her photo?"

"Maybe, but she was very ordinary looking. Absolutely forgettable, nothing that would distinguish her in a crowd really." I nodded in agreement though I thought the lady had been pretty.

"Thank you both. I have made a full report of your experience, and if you will wait a few minutes I will have it typed up for you to read and sign." Dixon opened his wallet and took out a business card and started to hand it to GG. Then he pulled it back and turned it over and wrote on the back with his pen. "This is my cell number if you remember anything else," then he handed it to GG. "In the meantime, please just sit and wait."

"Oh, DI Dixon do you suppose it would be possible for us to have some refreshment? A couple of Pepsi with ice?"

"Absolutely," he said with a nod. "I will return shortly." As he exited the room GG said, "Dick Tracy, that's what I will call him." Then she looked at me and added, "He was a famous detective."GG sat back in her chair, still smiling.

GG likes to give names to strangers, usually the names of famous people or characters. She told me that giving everyone a name made her feel like everyone was a friend. And you would never feel lonely.I could tell she wanted to remove her shoes again. So to tease her I bent over and looked right at her feet. She shrugged and smiled back. Then she said, "This room is ghastly. They need to provide some magazines and maybe even a television if they expect people to wait around. I hope they type fast. I am getting tired and hungry." And grouchy too, I thought.

At that moment, the same tubby little man that had shown us in earlier pushed through the door and quickly set two small paper cups of water on the table. With a big smile, he said, "Here we go, Pepsi with ice." Then he turned and left.

GG turned to me, and we both started giggling. Then picking up our flimsy cups we made a toast. Cheers.

GG's breakfast room was bright with the morning sun. Done in shades of buttercup and cream, with colorful flower embroidery along the edges of the table linen, it was like a storybook.

GG told me she used her fancy things even when alone, but especially enjoyed sharing them. She believed starting your day with pretty things was a good investment in good cheer and felt it set a high standard for the day. That is a nice idea, but not sure if it works when you are grabbing a bowl of Fruit Loops before heading off to school?

GG sat complaining about the lack of food and no newspaper while I was looking over the goodies and thinking there seemed to be plenty to eat.

"Rose has gone up north to see her family, and I forgot to tell her that we were not going to Switzerland," GG said as she poked a pastry in the basket. "I also forgot to tell the Porters to restart the newspapers. I will take care of that today."

GG perked up and added, "It somehow does seem a bit nicer to start the day without all of that nasty news about sleazy politicians and celebrities in rehab." GG decided to risk it and reached in the basket of yesterday's pastry and dug out a brioche. It was perfect, which surprised her, so she had two with jam. So did I.

After our breakfast we dressed. When we met in the entry hall we both abruptly stopped and assessed each other. I had appeared in a pink and black western shirt, with rhinestone buttons and black buckskin pants.

"Holy cow!" GG shook her head.

I looked down at GG's feet. She had on a crazy tall pair of blue shoes that I was certain was a bad choice, so I pointed at them and said, "Holy cow back at ya."

"Point taken from the shoe police. Oh, we need to get going; we can figure out your Calamity Jane wardrobe later."

"The iconic image of London is just 15 minutes from our doorstep. Do you know what that is?" GG quizzed cheerfully as we paced along the river walk.

"Sure, and I can't wait to take a ride."

"Ride? That's not possible." GG shifted me to the inside of the sidewalk. The traffic was zooming by just inches from the outer edge, and it was always GG's fear that a car would jump the curb.

"Why, is it broken?" I was skipping along, unaware of my grandmothers repositioning.

"Huh? What's broken? I know Disney has turned just about everything into a ride, but there is no way to turn a bell into a ride."

"What bell? I was talking about the Ferris wheel. The really big one."

"Big Ben is the icon, not the tacky London Eye," GG said, curling her lip in distaste. That horrible thing should have never have been allowed. Ok, maybe down the river somewhere near the docklands, but never in view of Parliament." With disgust GG added, "A blight on the heart of the city." But a fun one, I thought.

Ok, so she really doesn't like the Eye, but I want a ride. It might be tricky, but I figured I could find just the right approach. Smiling, but serious, "It seems to me that riding a Ferris wheel would be more fun than looking at a bell, even a very special bell."

"Oh, we don't actually get to see the bell, we get to see the Queen Elizabeth Bell Tower and the clock."

"GG, you cannot tell me you would rather look at a bell building than to take a fun ride? That doesn't sound at all like you," I added.

"No, I don't suppose it does." GG frowned. She didn't want to seem boring. "I guess we have time to do both, but I really should have worn my flat shoes to go on a carnival ride."

"GG, you always wear shoes that hurt your feet. That seems pretty silly to me. Will you please promise not to do that?" I left my cowboy hat at home, so next time you can leave those tall shoes," I bargained.

"Oh, ok, I will not wear shoes that hurt my feet." GG raised her hand as if giving an oath.

Getting near the Eye, GG spotted a red London phone box. "Abby, I recently read because of all the cell phones the red phone boxes are destined for extinction. Step inside the box. I want to get your photo while these iconic boxes can still be found."

GG quickly snapped my picture with her phone, then took my arm and pulled me out of the red box. She then grabbed a wet-wipe from her bag and thrust it into my hand.

"Here honey, use this." Quite used to my grandmother's germ and grime phobia, I did as told without comment.

Standing in the long line for the London Eye I said, "Look, GG, you can save £5.00 just for being over 60." Several women standing nearby snickered and looked away.

Horrified but cold faced, GG replied, "What good news; perhaps when I turn sixty we can come back and benefit from that generous offer."

"Daddy said you were sixty-something, I think," I said trying to refresh my grandmother's memory. Another important thing, and it is big, is GG gets really cranky if anyone mentions her age or even says the word birthday. Sometimes when she actually has to tell her age she will just make up any old number like she did with Dick Tracy. I figured out she must have had something very bad happen to her on her birthday. Maybe she had a big party and none of her friends came. Or she had a beautiful cake and it fell on the floor and the dog ate it. Whatever happened, it still makes her crabby to remember it. I don't bring it up, but unfortunately sometimes others do, and that makes steam come out of her ears. "Never mind about that, it is our turn next," said GG who insisted on paying the full price.

The ride on the London Eye was slow and did give a remarkable view of the vast city. GG even bought the souvenir photo that was offered at the end. We didn't look very good in it, but it was a cool photo.

"Now I am hungry. Where shall we have lunch? Scalari or Lagan's?"

"They both sound pretty fancy, GG. Can we just this once have lunch someplace where you don't kiss the waiters?" My face was pulled in a knot.

"Dear, I don't kiss waiters, they kiss me, and it is just a way they greet their favorite guests." GG stood straight and flicked imaginary lint from her skirt.

"Well, they have a lot of favorites because they seem to kiss everyone." I was not backing down.

"Yes, everyone that actually gets in the door is a favorite. You have to be a favorite to get a reservation."

"Then why do you give them money?" I persisted because I did not want a fancy lunch that required me to sit for two hours.

"I am certainly not giving them money for a kiss; I am giving them money for a table."

"Is the food better at those tables?" I argued while clearly teasing her.

"I'm on to you, kiddo, you are just winding me up. So yes, everything is better." She laughed, "But you can win this one." We shared a tasty pizza from a chain, and no one was kissed.

After lunch we crossed the Thames River on the Millennium Footbridge. There are great views up and down the river. "Look, GG, are we near where that lady threw the gun and our camera in?"

"Yes, sweetie, very near. I wish we had our camera so we could take some wide photos like everyone else seems to be doing. My phone camera will have to do."

"Do you think the detective is trying to find out what happened?"

"Maybe we should call him?"

Next we were off on what GG called a whistle-stop tour, or just a quick peek at quite a few things. First we visited the National Gallery and took their highlights tour. We saw paintings by Van Gogh, Leonardo Da Vinci, Renoir, and many more. They were beautiful, and some I had even seen in books. I bought an umbrella with sunflowers like the Van Gogh painting, as it had started to sprinkle outside.

GG told me she knew from raising my Dad that children preferred to do things rather than see things, but these superior exhibits were important and she felt they should not be missed. They were pretty neat, but after a while they started all to look alike. As we were leaving the Victoria and Albert Museum GG said, "Now I believe it is time for some treats." I nodded in agreement. "I know you don't like shopping, but could I tempt you with Hamley?"

"Yippee, you sure can." Hamley proclaimed to be the biggest and oldest toy store in the world and was located nearby on Regent Street, but I could tell her feet hurting and that was confirmed when she yelled, "Taxi!"

At Hamley I would not be rushed. I insisted we walk each floor before making my selections. "GG, Penny loves this store and it makes me miss her to be here."

"She does love this place. When you and your Dad went to Venice we spent a whole day here and at the

Harrods Toy Kingdom."

"Yeah, I remember she had loads of new toys and a drum set too, which I know my Dad thought was a bad idea."

"We will have to find her a special gift. But you have certainly earned one too for your consistent cooperation and good manners." Glad to know it was noticed, I thought.

On the third floor we abruptly halted and both stared into a bin with a selection of plastic guns. This reminded us of the strange incident on the boat. "GG, I wonder if they every found that gun in the water?"

"I wonder if Dick Tracy ever bothered to look?"

GG loves to do all the girlie stuff, so our last stop of the day was a beauty spa where we each had a mani-pedi as they served us beverages and snacks. I picked my favorite color, turquoise blue, for my nails and GG picked red.

While at the spa GG told me she positively could not function or keep up with me unless she was well-rested, and an early night was a must. I was still on California time so I was more than ready for my pillow.

"Good morning, GG, what does London have in store for us today?" I asked while I poured myself a glass of chocolate milk.

GG was now vigorously raking a brush through her thick hair, scraping every strand as if it were cookie batter being gathered from a mixing bowl. I looked at GG and wondered how she had any hair left with that brutal brushing.

"Tonight let's see a play, musical, of course." Then she held out the brush as if offering me a go. I shook my head.

"Of course." I was looking around for a banana for my yogurt.

"Darling, get the Time-Out magazine from the rack." GG tapped her finger in the direction of the magazines. "Let's take a look at our choices."

I jumped up as asked and reached into the rack and pulled out the magazine. The front cover was a large, colorful advertisement with the young boy jumping. "How about Billy Elliott?" I asked, pointing to the picture.

"No. Too much smutty language; I saw it twice and it was very offensive." Twice, I thought? I continued to flip the colorful pages. "How about Stomp?"

"Good grief, now really Abby, does that sound at all like anything I would enjoy? The very word stomp is annoying to me."

"No, I guess not. I give up, what do you want to see?" I knew my bossy grandmother would already have something in mind.

"I think you would like Mamma Mia."

"Again? Didn't we see that in New York?"

"Sweetie, fine musicals are like operas, you can watch them many times; in fact it is expected." She said this with authority as if she was giving a lecture to a room of students.

"So Mamma Mia it is." I shrugged.

"I wish we had time to listen to the music right now." GG turned and looked me over. "Ok, sweetie, out of your pjs and we will be on our way".

I had debuted another of my western ensembles. This one was a quilted patchwork skirt and matching jacket — a coat of many colors. "These aren't my pjs, I bought them for our trip. Very cozy and I like it." I wasn't backing down quite yet.

"Ok, Annie Oakley, then I am going to wear my new red shoes." Another bad choice, I thought. Our sartorial bargain agreed, we were soon out the door and on our way.

"Westminster Abbey is a true landmark, mega famous."

"It looks old," I said.

"Positively ancient, but they take good care of the place. And we are in luck, because they have an exceptional Verger tour, which I have booked."

"What's a Verger tour?" To me it sounded like a ride.

"The Abbey is a church, and the Vergers are men who help the priests and ministers. Such as giving lucky visitors like us a tour."

We joined a group of about 20 people and headed off. There were a few other children on the tour, and I smiled at them. With elbows tucked to her side, one of the girls waved at me. This tour was a good idea as it allowed us to avoid the scrum of tourists, who all looked confused and lost in the cavernous place. Only GG didn't look lost; she had been here many times.

"You sure like churches, GG. I bet we have been to a hundred of them."

Relishing her role as tour guide and educator, GG patted her guidebook and began adding more Cathedral facts. "Yes, I do like churches. Also mosques, temples, and shrines. They always make me feel that the people who built them and the people that visit them are somehow connected. That way you are never a stranger and you are part of history."

The tour was historical, all about queens and kings in the past and also famous statesmen and authors. Some were names I had heard before: Jane Austen, Winston Churchill, Sir Isaac Newton, and Rudyard Kipling. I took out a small tablet and pen that I had purchased at the Tower gift shop two days before and started to make notes. I wanted to remember to tell my teachers.

After the tour and a stop at the gift shop, we walked to nearby St James Park in front of Buckingham Palace and fed half a loaf of stale bread to the already overstuffed water fowl. GG took the opportunity to plop on a bench and rest her feet. She kicked off her shoes and sighed loudly while I scattered the bread.

She placed our small packages on the ground nearby and when I finished feeding the ducks I sat on a small scrub of grass, raised my knees to my chest, and circled my shins with my arms. Very relaxed, I kicked off my shoes and smiled at GG.

"Do those shoes hurt?" she teased.

"No, sweetheart, I'm just chill-axing," I said, clearly trying to imitate her voice. This made her laugh. She arched her back and gave her whole body a stretch.

"Good plan."

At just that moment a young boy ran up beside our bench and grabbed GG's handbag, which she had left on the ground with the packages at her feet. He took off running, and GG lurched up and took off after him.

I hastily scooped up our shoes and took off too. GG was screaming, "Stop, thief!"

I played softball for a couple of years, so I reared back and flung a shoe and hit the boy in the shoulder, which caused him to slow. He looked back at me with a scowl, but he kept running. Then I launched another shoe. This time one of GG's shoes got him right on his ear and the high heel made a gash. It started to bleed. He grabbed his ear, turned, and glared at me. Then he circled, bent down, and picked up the shoe that had torn his ear and with a great right arm flung it into the duck pond. He kept going.

GG wasn't going very fast, as she was barefoot and the path was rocky. I was still carrying two shoes when I finally caught the wily scoundrel and grabbed at the bag. In my fury I gave the kid a swift kick. Then he kicked me back, which hurt and caused me to let go. He took off just as GG caught up with us.

GG also hollered some harsh words while she grabbed her purse strap and tugged. I reached for the boy and again fought on. The boy kicked out but missed me, and then he grabbed my ponytail and held on. GG tugged hard on her bag, and the kid stumbled and rolled right into the mucky duck pond, still holding my ponytail. I went right in with him. It was icky and freezing cold.

"The splashes and the yelling had raised a crowd. In the scuffle the contents of the purse flew up, and GG's wallet was caught mid-air by another boy that had joined the fracas. He grabbed the wallet and a shopping bag with items from the Abbey gift shop and took off in another direction. In a pincer move he circled GG's right flank, grabbed her other shoe, which I had dropped, and he flung that one as well into the slimy water. It was chaos.

The boy was trying to get out of the water, and so was I.

But the pond scum was slick, and we both slipped and fell back. GG had not given up and soon had hold of the boy that threw her other shoe in. She was tugging and trying to shake her wallet and shopping bag loose; they were going in circles.

Two adults and several other children rushed up and started shaking GG loose, and the boy took off with her wallet. GG was practically hysterical and hit out at one of the women and yelled, "What do you think you are doing? That pygmy thug stole my purse. My money!" With hair aflame, GG was in a veritable fireball.

The others, faces fierce were now shouting, which sounded very hostile, but with everyone shouting at once I wasn't entirely certain what was being said.

I scrambled ashore just as a policeman arrived. I was certain he would help. However, the others gathered had told the policeman that GG had been seen kicking, hitting, and cursing a small local boy and they wanted her arrested. GG was still flailing and twirling, and the policeman started to get angry with her.

By this time one boy was long gone, but the boy from the pond was clinging to one of the adults. He said I pushed him in and he was acting like he was frightened, but I looked right at him and he smirked.

I was dripping and covered in green pond scum, and we had no shoes. The officer walked us to a kiosk in the park and took our statement. "I hope you are not going to arrest us. We know an important detective, and he will tell you we are not bad," I said.

"A detective?" asked the officer.

"That's right, said GG patting, her soggy handbag. "We are

assisting Scotland Yard in a major investigation. I have his card here somewhere."

I looked at GG and hoped she didn't embellish too much more. "We were just trying to get her purse back."

"You are not allowed to hit children, Madame, but no, we are not going to arrest you. Either of you." The officer winked at me. "That family of pickpockets and purse snatchers has been causing trouble in several of the Royal Parks. Sign here and you can be on your way."

On the taxi ride home GG said, "I don't feel much like going to a play tonight."

"The only place I want to go is in the shower," I replied. We looked each other over, and my gaze stopped at our feet. They were bare and dirty, and the efforts and expense of our recent manicures and pedicures long lost. Her gypsy-red nails and my turquoise ones mocked us.

GG loved ancient churches, but she did not mention going to St Paul's Cathedral. I was suspicious. It was because the guidebook said we could climb the 528 steps to the top of the dome, and I knew GG would want no part of that.

Instead she took me to Westminster Cathedral, the Roman Catholic heart of England, and we took the elevator to the top of the bell tower for an amazing view of the city. We were up there alone, and it was pretty small, so soon we were headed to the ground again.

"Time to light some candles?" I asked. GG nodded.

"Yes. And I have heard they have an angel tour, and that sounds like fun," she said as we approached the information desk.

"Oh no, GG, it looks like I am not old enough for the tour," I said, disappointed as I pointed to a sign that said you must be ten.

"How ridiculous," said GG, "much older than you are and you would have quit believing in angels. Don't fret; we will do our own tour."

"How do we do that?"

"Let us see how many angels we can spot. The one who sees the most will win."

"Win what?" I said, looking about hoping to start spotting soon.

"That's easy, we shall go to the shop and buy an angel for the winner." In most places there is a gift shop waiting.

We wandered around the enormous old church listening to the choir singing while looking at gargoyles and collecting angels for our contest. "That is eight for me and eleven for you, Abby."

"Victory is sweet, but I think that one by the big stained glass window may have been a flying cat."

"Even without that one you still won. Congratulations."

"Look, there is a place to light candles." I pointed to a quiet corner. "We can light one for Grandpa Ted like we always do?"

"Oh yes, and another one just to say thank you for our little trips."

We approached the small side chapel area and GG got out money for the candles. The large metal coin box was elegantly perched on a small stand near the candle altar.

GG folded a large bill to push through the slot, and when she tried, it got stuck. Trying to maintain her calm and contemplative composure at this holy ritual, she tried to gently jiggle the cash though the opening. It would not budge. The bill was half in and half out. GG gave it one more vigorous shove and dislodged the whole box from the stand and it went flying. As it crashed to the hard marble floor the lid sprang open and the money inside, which was mostly coins, went bouncing in all directions.

"Abby, quick help me pick these up," said GG as she bent over and began gathering coins. There were far too many to hold in our hands, so we started stuffing money in our pockets. We continued in the curled shrimp-like position and had scooped most of the money from the floor when we turned slightly and I noticed a pair of black brogues and the folds and hem of a black cassock swished into view. We slowly rose up to a standing position. We were silent. "May I be of some assistance?" softly asked the pious-faced elderly priest while looking right at our full hands and pockets.

"I-I-er, I Father," stuttered a horrified GG. I kept quiet while shakily I began pulling the money from my jacket. Then I thrust it toward the man.

"I accidentally, I didn't mean," I bleated out.

"Here," GG offered several hands full of cash and coins. "And a little extra too." She had pulled out her wallet and was giving the man a wad of money.

"Just a misunderstanding, then?" said the comely priest.

"Exactly," I offered. "We have a lot of those."

"I need a break, and I know a great place for lunch," GG

said as we walked back out of the Cathedral into the soft sunlight.

"Yes, I could use a break too. I thought that pastor was going to have us arrested again."

"Not again. We have not been arrested. Remember we were the victims yesterday and today; well, it wasn't our fault."

I didn't feel like much arguing about blame so I asked, "Ok, where is this great place?"

"The Serpentine in Hyde Park."

"I hope that family of thieves hasn't moved over there?" I was just teasing, but I did hope it was true.

"Well, if they are we will be ready for them this time. Now let's find a ..."

"Taxi," I shouted and started to wave as one had just come into view.

We were seated at an outdoor table near the water. It was a bit breezy, but a rare London day without rain, so GG told me we were lucky. The ducks were gabbing away, and I hoped their chatter did not remind GG of the purse-snatcher the previous day. Then she spoke up. "Abby, sorry about that misunderstanding yesterday. Stuff like that can happen in a big city. It is just the kind of thing that makes your Dad cross. Perhaps we should keep this to ourselves?"

"Sure, no problem. All on the DL."

"DL?" GG was baffled.

"Yeah, the Down Low, a secret."

"We don't keep secrets, but DL really? Why are you talking like that?" She sounded slightly irritated.

"Like I am 9? It sort of comes natural." That probably sounded sarcastic.

"No, like some rap star. What next? Going to let your jeans fall off your toochie?" GG smiled.

"I think that is only boys. Have you ever listened to any hip...," end of conversation on urban music. GG abruptly picked up her menu card that was under a rock and started to read.

A rather plumpish doughy-faced young girl with a perky manner stopped at our table. "I am not your server, but I can take your drink orders."

"Root beer for me," I said. The girl shook her head. "Ok, lemonade."

"Make that two." Then the girl smiled at me and said, "Cute outfit; is that from America?"

"Yes," I replied with a smug smile as I turned toward GG. "I picked it out myself." GG raised her eyebrows really high and rolled her eyes.

GG knows my friends from her visits to Santa Barbara, so while we waited for our food she started quizzing me on what everyone was up to. "Did Camden ever get his puppy?"

"Yep. They call him Neptune because every time they go out on their fishing boat he jumps overboard. They had to buy him a life vest." This made GG laugh.

"For a dog? I have never heard of such a thing. Did Lauren cut her beautiful hair? I hope not."

I shook my head. "No, and it is really long now. No one wants her to cut it, but it is her hair so I guess she can do what she wants.

"Kora got a new horse, Bella, and she got thrown off." I waved my arms to show it was a wild fall, then raised my elbow. "Now she has a purple cast on her broken arm."

"Ouch, that sounds painful; is she afraid now?"

"Kora afraid of horses? No chance. She would stand up on the saddle and ride like a circus performer if her mom would let her."

"Doesn't Brooke ride too?"

"Yes, she's real good at it. She loves to ride. So far she hasn't broken anything."

"Thank heavens for that. What's Nathan up to?"

"OMG, he does karate and he even got a belt. It is positively awesome."

"Wow, impressive. That must take a lot of hard work."

"Their cat Reese had nine kittens. Their mom Julie said they could only keep one, so they are looking for homes. I'm helping. You like cats, GG, do you want one, they come in all colors?" I held my hands out in as if doing a commercial on TV.

She shook her head. "I love cats, but I travel too much to actually have one of my own."

"I am asking everyone. Camille said she wants one for her birthday, and I think her mom might let her because their cat is old."

"Don't count him out yet; cats can live a long time."

"Brody?"

"No, he has a big dog."

"Did you try Wesley? They like animals."

"Wesley and Sydney both want one, but their mom said they might eat her chickens."

"Oh, that does sound risky. Eric?" I did not reply, instead, just shook my head.

"That's about it, GG. Everyone asks me when you are coming back? Especially Camden, he likes your snacks."

"It's nice to be remembered, even if it is for your croissants." GG smiled and picked up her sandwich. Guess that wrapped up the kid talk.

We were ready to go, but the waiter was not nearby. He had previously left the bill, so GG just put the money on the table and we departed by the water path.

We were strolling at a leisurely pace discussing our next stops, when we were almost out of view from the cafe and we heard a loud commotion behind us. We stopped and wheeled to see what was happening.

Fast approaching was our waiter, the bistro manager, and a policeman. "Not again," I said shaking my head.

"Don't be silly, that has nothing to do with us," said GG turning back in the direction of the taxi stand. But I wasn't so sure and soon we found out that GG was very mistaken.

"Dine and dash! That is outrageous," GG flared, her hands held high in protection. "Don't you dare touch me or this child." She turned and started to fumble for her phone after having been ordered by the policeman to stop.

"Ma'am, this man tells me you left his establishment without paying for your service. Is that true?"

"Not only is it not true, it is slander! That beast probably stole the money himself," said the inflamed GG giving the men a furious look. She looked really mad.

"She did pay, I saw her," I offered quietly.

"GG turned and scowled at the men while waiting for her call to be answered.

"Yesterday when we got arrested GG told them we know a famous detective, and maybe she is calling him?"

"Arrested?" asked the policeman.

"No, we were not," GG said as she turned her attention back to her phone. "Oh Detective Dixon, I am so happy to reach you."

"Me? GG Gable. We met a few days ago over the gun incident on the boat." GG said this loud so the men could hear.

"There is a bit of a misunderstanding here in Hyde Park, and I was hoping you might help? Will you please tell the police officer we are not criminals?" I was nodding my head to show support.

"No, we haven't been arrested yet, but could you please?" Then GG thrust the phone toward the policeman. "Here."

It took about 10 minutes for all parties to cool off and for an agreement to be reached. Detective Dixon had offered a character reference, and the officer was satisfied. It was agreed GG had not left without paying and perhaps the wind had blown away her payment and generous tip. She then agreed that to settle the matter she would pay again, but they must apologize for their accusations, which they happily did.

In the taxi on the way home, GG gave me a cuddle and whispered, "Abby, I think we need to add this misunderstanding to the DL list."

"The DL list it is."

GG had not once yet taken me to a restaurant where the waiters kissed you, or to Harrods to shop. However, the week was soon ending, and she told me she just could not send me home without showing me off at her favorite haunts.

The next morning at breakfast she announced, "I woke up today with the overwhelming urge to have Eggplant Parmesan. What about you, Abby, doesn't that sound delicious?" She took a sip of her coffee and smiled at me over the brim of her cup.

"Not for breakfast, but for lunch it sounds ok." I picked up a croissant and drizzled on some honey. "I bet there is just one place in all of London that serves the best. Am I right?" I took a nibble. Then turned to GG with smiling eyes and lips puckered for a big smooch. From a nearby chair I picked up the angel I had won at the cathedral. "Kiss, kiss," I said as I laid a big, noisy kiss on the stuffed toy.

"You are a very clever girl," said GG as she puckered up and grabbed the angel and she too gave it a big kiss. "In the spirit of cooperation, what would you like to do today before we go to Scalari?"

"I don't think my eyeballs can take anymore art or old bits of wood and old rugs and stuff in museums. Maybe we should go to Harrods?"

"Oh yes, excellent." GG looked like I had flipped a light switch inside her.

"I would like to get some presents for Daddy and Penny, my Mom too if that's ok? She likes Harrods almost as much as you do."

"Of course you can get your Mom a present. Presents

for everyone."

GG wanted to tell me to get dressed fancy for our final day, but she had all but given up on that conversation. She had started referring to my clothes as my Dollywood couture.

I stood smiling before GG in a chamois fringed skirt and matching fringed vest with a diamante embossed star over the heart. I had a ruffled white blouse with pink bolo tie. She looked at me and rolled her eyes.

"This is a perfect agenda, and I am going to wear my new emerald shoes."

"Those really tall ones? Yikes. They don't hurt your feet, do they? Remember, you promised."

"They felt like clouds when I put them on in the store, but anything is possible." GG was hedging the question in a fun way. "Anyway, they are new, and Scalari is the perfect audience for their maiden voyage. I'm willing to risk it." Then she sank comfortably into an easy chair in the den.

I sat down on the floor and continued to drink my orange juice. "With our relaxed schedule today we have time to kick back and watch some morning television." GG reached for a basket of remotes.

She says she hates electronics, but her television was the biggest one I had ever seen in someone's house. It filled up the whole wall. Device in hand, GG looked at it like she had never seen it before. She waited a few seconds and I thought she was going to give up before she even turned it on, but soon she begin to channel surf. She landed on the news, and in exactly the same instance we both shouted, "It's her!"

Fumbling with the controls she had muted the sound

and was now trying to get the audio back on. She dropped the controller to the rug, and I picked it up and pushed the mute release. We saw the gun woman from the boat speaking.

"Today on the steps of the Old Bailey Court House I must sadly acknowledge the case against the notorious gangster in the gangland-style killing of his enemy was today dropped after the murder weapon could not be produced by the Crown Prosecution. The Defense has demanded all charges be dropped and that if the police had ever had the gun they claimed to have in evidence, that it would have been produced in court today. We will continue in our efforts to remove this violent man and his nefarious crew from the streets of London."

"This is all very confusing, Abby. Is she a lawyer or a reporter?"

"No GG, I think she is a policewoman, and that doesn't make sense at all." I shook my head.

It took us a moment to realize what was actually going on. "Abby, we must go back to Scotland Yard at once. Do you remember where I put the card with DI Dixon's number on it?" GG was shifting her head and looking around as if she had somehow just dropped the card.

I jumped up and bounded out of the room. Returning quickly with the card I had located in GG's purse, I thrust the card toward my grandmother. "What now?"

GG dialed the cell number, and it went to voice mail. "DI Dixon, we know who dropped the gun; we saw the woman from the boat on TV. We are coming to your office." My heart was pounding, and I think GG's was as well because she was almost breathless as she called the main number on the front of the card and also relayed her message to a desk sergeant, who told her DI Dixon was in court. She was also told he was due to return to his office in about an hour.

"Perfect, Abby. Now there is a very good prospect of apprehending the horrible woman from the boat."

"She is sure going to be surprised."

"I suspect she will be shocked. Now we have plenty of time to get dressed properly. I plan to enjoy the process of my lovely lotions and potions, so do help me out this chair. I seemed to have sunk in." I took GG's arms and gave her a tug. We both made groaning noises, then started laughing as I fell to the floor.

We returned to the huge reception area at Scotland Yard and briskly went to the head of the line. "I am GG Gable, and I have an appointment with DI Dixon. Please buzz me in," GG said with her usual authority.

"I am sorry, ma'am, your name is not on the list. Please wait over in the seating area, and the kid cannot go in."

"She's 19."

"I'm 19." We replied in unison.

"And no, I will not take a seat. I have come about the gangster murder, and I do not intend to wait while you fiddle with your list." GG was on a mission. The officer waved over two uniformed men with guns who then escorted us to the seating area. The mission would have to wait.

We sat in grey plastic tub chairs and waited. GG was thinking her skirt was getting wrinkled, and she began furiously tapping her foot. I joined her in tapping. When the door finally buzzed open, the chubby man that had given us the water stuck his head out and waved us in. He didn't bother to discourage my entry and escorted us to a different but identical grey room, where he told us to be seated.

"They kind of like grey around here," I said.

"Yes, another ghastly grey room, they must have gotten the paint on sale," laughed GG. Twenty minutes had passed and still no one had come.

I was jumpy and anxious, and this small grey room was getting smaller. Just when I was thinking GG was ready to bolt and take us from this cell, the door opened and in sauntered Dick Tracy. Seconds later, walking a few steps behind him was the woman from the boat. GG's head jerked and her eyebrows shot skyward. My eyes were frozen wide with astonishment. Everything stopped; we were stunned still.

Before either of us could say anything DI Dixon said, "This is Sergeant Snow. She is the co-investigator on the case you mentioned. Now tell us what has brought you here today?"

GG was still silent with shock, which for her was quite rare. The color had drained from her face. And my tummy was whirling. Halted by surprise and apprehension, we were not sure how to proceed. I remained still and silent, but was certain the woman knew who we were.

"My granddaughter is leaving town tomorrow, and I just wanted to know if there was anything else you needed from her before she departed?" GG's fear was audible as her voice sounded funny.

My Dad once told me GG often resorted to playing dumb

when it benefited her. She is intelligent and well-educated, but used this ploy to her advantage here as she shook her head as if it were an empty salt shaker and continued bright-eyed, "If not, we will just be on our jolly way. We have reservations at Scalari, and we don't want them to give our table away." I managed to shake my head as if agreeing.

The quickness of her answers surprised them, but GG wanted us out of there. She jumped up awkwardly and grabbed me by the hand. She began moving us toward the door of the small room, ready to make our getaway.

"Are you absolutely certain that is all?" asked the woman in an openly sinister tone. I barely controlled the urge to shiver. "There isn't anything at all you would like to say or ask?"

I turned and faced her with a glare. "Yes, there is something," I said, now emboldened. "Would you happen to know where we might get a new camera? Ours seems to have gone for a swim."

GG was horrified at my outburst and pulled me into her arms. I could feel her heart was thumping. It was time to go.

I knew GG did want to speak to Detective Dixon, but she did not know how she could get him alone. Then with a calm she did not feel she said, "Abby come on, sweetie, Scalari is waiting. Oh DI Dixon, if you haven't tried Scalari you really must. It can be most rewarding." I hoped that Dixon would get the hint and that she had not made it too obvious.

Scalari was crowded, noisy, and quite welcoming. Vincenzo

and Marco were effusive with kisses and compliments and seated us in the best table in the restaurant. GG was smiling and seemed to have forgotten about the police, but then she said, "We are a party of three." She was hoping DI Dixon took the hint and would soon join us. However, after we had eaten most of our lunch he had not yet appeared. I had the lobster spaghetti, and it was so good I ate every bite.

GG did not want to alarm me, so she avoided conversation about what had happened at the police station, but I wanted to know. I also wanted to cheer her up so I said, "We have been pretty lucky. It only rained one day this week."

"Yes, maybe it is evidence of global warming? I know the Brits will be happy if it is." She picked up the remaining olive from her plate and popped it in her mouth. She signaled the waiter to bring dessert menus.

"You must try the tiramisu. It is divine." GG licked her lips.

"Devine is good. Sure, I will try that." GG nodded to the waiter, and he went off to get our sweets.

My curiosity was getting to me so I asked, "Well, GG, do you think DI Dixon is going to figure this all out?"

"Hard to say, he didn't let on that he knew who she was. And I had rather hoped he would show up by now. Let's forget about her; where shall we go on our next trip?" This change of subject brightened GG, as this is always a happy conversation between us. We were starting to relax.

GG snapped to alert and cut me short when she heard Marco saying, "Yes, please follow me. Madame Gable has been waiting for you." Finally.

We looked around, expecting to see Dick Tracey and were horrified to see Sergeant Snow heading our way.

"Abby, I have no time to explain. Quickly, you must go upstairs and wait at a table up there and do not come down. I will come get you as soon as I can. Go now."

I rarely heard my grandmother speak so commandingly and knew then that I must do as asked without any questions or delay.

Just then DC Snow arrived and was seated. Marco offered her a drink and GG was astonished that she said yes, and she even reached over and picked up a bread stick.

"What a nice surprise," said a very nervous GG.

With barely disguised envy and contempt, Snow looked around the room. Smartly dressed people, jewels, with time and money to spare.

She hissed, "Not nice at all, but I do believe you are surprised. Expecting Dixon, were you?" sneered the Sergeant. "Shall we cut the chitchat? You have been sticking your nose in where it doesn't belong."

GG anxiously raised her hand to her nose. "Busybodies like you are usually laughed at and ignored at the Met, but probably because you are stinkin' rich you got more attention than most of the nutters that come in," Snow spat oozing disgust. "My friends are not at all pleased with the story you told police, and I am going to have to insist you shut up."

The woman's sinister words chilled GG to the very core. "Sure thing. Consider it done." GG waved a bejeweled hand as if shooing away a pesky fly. "No problem. Abby is leaving for California, and I am thinking I might like a change of scenery too. So there, problem solved." GG was pushing the cheery tone and hoped to reassure this evil woman.

"Not quite solved. Not good enough. I want you to go back

to the Yard and change your story. You did not see a gun. Tell them the sun was in your eyes or you were showing off to your granddaughter or something."

"Surely Dixon will not believe me."

"Then tell him you are old and forget things."

GG was too frightened to react to this insult. "I guess I could try, but I can't guarantee it will work." Her unsteady hand reached for her water glass as a waiter delivered a beverage for Snow.

I had not gone upstairs, as GG had instructed. Instead, I had gone around the corner and asked Marco to call the police. I told him the lady with GG was very bad. I stood with him as we eyed the two at the table.

"Just tell him. While you do that, I will go upstairs and wait with the little princess. After all, I am a police officer; she will be safe with me," she said with intentional menace.

GG shot out of her chair. She turned bright red and totally unalarmed by her own daring against this vile woman. She was positively incandescent with fury at the very idea of DS being near me. As GG jumped, her back stiffened and she braced for a fight. I tried to run to help her, but Marco held my arm.

"Oh no you don't! Get out!" GG bellowed in Snow's face. As she stood up, she knocked the table over and sent beverages and our divine dessert tumbling to the floor with a loud crash. GG wailed, "Vincenzo! Call the police!"

"That will not be necessary; they are here already," announced Dick Tracey as he came around the corner of the entry and into the premier dining area of Scalari. I was right behind him.

He put his arm out to steady a very shaky GG. She would later remember it as a cuddle. "We have been suspicious of Sergeant Snow for some time now, and the look on your face when she entered the interrogation room was all the confirmation we needed."

"Wa-what took you so long?" I asked fighting back tears. I had been so worried that Sergeant Snow would harm GG.

"We needed to retrieve the CCTV footage of DS Snow exiting the boat, and just a few minutes ago the divers recovered the gun from the muddy bottom of the Thames, exactly where you said it was dropped."

GG sank to her chair, put her arms across the disheveled table, bent her head down, and laid it across her arms and sighed deeply. I thought she was going to cry, so I put my hand on her shoulder.

The restaurant had earlier gone quiet, but now people slowly resumed conversation and eating while the waiters were delicately trying to clean the mess GG had created.

DI Dixon put his hand under GG's chin and lifted her face. "Chin up. The gangster murder prosecution can go forward, and we have you to thank and you too, Miss Abigail." GG replied to him with a huge smile. "We will have a police car standing by outside to take you home when you have finished your lunch."

Dixon patted GG's arm and turned to depart, but just before he did, he winked at GG's now upturned face. She blushed as he moved to join DS Snow who was now in handcuffs and being led out by two officers.

GG, revived by the flattery, grabbed me. "Abby! Are you ok?" She was certain I would be terrified. I wan't scare, I had been angry. Now I was so happy to be hugging my grandmother. We were safe and we were heroes.

The police car pulled to the entrance of my grandmother's building and out we tumbled. Waving goodbye to the police officers as our ride from Scalari pulled away, we gave each other more hugs and were animatedly walking up the building steps hand in hand.

"Abby, we are heroes. We are big time crime fighters now." GG's mind was a veritable Mardi Gras. She saw herself in a Wonder Woman outfit being asked by the police to solve more crimes. "This is thrilling. I wish we could tell your Dad."

"Tell me what?" said a familiar voice. We looked at each other, then turned to see my Dad, who had just emerged from a taxi.

"Daddy!"

"Hi, Cupcake," he said as he swept me in his outstretched arms.

"Wheels, what are you doing in London?" GG asked without really wanting to know.

"Mother, what are you doing in London?

"Now, don't be silly son, I live here," she replied with a forced cheery tone.

"Yes, I know where you live, Mom. What do you wish you could tell me, and does it have anything to do with your police escort?" My Dad draped his arm around his mother. "You two were supposed to be in Switzerland." We were all on the steps now.

I smiled up at my Dad. Switzerland seemed so long ago.

His sudden appearance was making GG nervous, but I could tell she was really happy to see him. GG loves my Dad big time and seeing him made both of us feel more secure, but why was he here?

"Please, let's get inside, I am ready to drop, and will someone tell me what is going on. Why are you in London and I am afraid to ask again, but why have the police just brought you home?"

Continuing to ignore my Dad's questions as we waited for his luggage to be dislodged from the taxi, GG asked in a disingenuous manner, "Where is Penny? Will you be staying long?"

"PJ is with her Mother in Santa Barbara and I am, as you know, supposed to be in Hong Kong. I had gone there for a baby christening of one of my design colleagues. I was barely off the plane from my 13-hour flight when I heard your hotel in Geneva was in a terrorist siege. All the cell phone lines were shut down; I went directly to the airport and got the first flight to Switzerland. Which happened to be on Aeroflot and routed through Moscow."

"Oh my, that is a lot of frequent flyer miles," said GG with a positive spin on the turn of events.

"After 16 more hours I raced to your hotel, and when I arrived the incident was over and they were all back to business as usual. It really had only been some unhappy union workers and militant demonstrators and not terrorists."

"The hotel said you had never arrived. Naturally, I assumed you had actually gone to Cairo," he said with sarcasm.

"Oh son, I hope you did not go all the way to Egypt?" GG sounded quite concerned for any inconvenience. I knew my Dad would be furious if he had. We stepped into the elevator.

"No, I did not. I called your favorite hotel in Cairo, and they said you were not there. So I called Rose. It took me half a day to reach her; she is apparently traveling as well. She told me you had been in London all week. And now I am here."

"You know it is important we be informed of any changes of plans and location." Now my Dad sounded cross. As we walked into the flat GG just nodded, trying to look guilty, but I don't think she really was.

"Mother, maybe we should sort this out where I can sit down. I am exhausted and must get some sleep before we have to leave for California in the morning. You do realize, by the time we get back to Santa Barbara I will have been around the world in just a couple of days?"

I started explaining that we were famous heroes of Scotland Yard. As we moved into the den my Dad said he wanted all the details, then he plopped in a chair and kicked off his shoes. I looked over at GG sitting in a chair, and she had already kicked off her shoes, so I did too. What a family.

Florence, Italy

There I was again at Heathrow Airport, London. This place is gigantic. With five terminals to choose from, 87,000 employees, 260,000 people per day, and sixty-six million passengers a year jostling for space, I did not want to be in the wrong place. GG loved it here. To her it signaled something exciting was about to happen. And when GG was involved it usually did. Our Grand Tour continued.

There she was. I twirled around with my hair bouncing, and ran as fast as I could through the crowd to my grandmother. As usual, GG went all gooey and melty when she saw me come through the arrival doors. She quickly signed the release papers and gave me big cuddle. She always smells good.

From what I have heard from my friends, GG is not like everyone's grandmothers. She is notorious for having screwball adventures, but I think I am lucky because GG and I are great pals and our adventures are amazing. I am pretty easy to get along with and I know when things get a bit crazy, as they sometimes do with GG, it will all work out.

It was difficult to deny she always meant well, but for my Dad the endless complications these problems had caused to his own life had exhausted him. The last thing he told me before I boarded my plane was, "positively no misunderstandings."

"Don't touch that filthy glass, honey," GG said with alarm. She quickly dug in her purse and produced a packed of wet wipes. Some things never change.

She pushed out through the glass doors of the airport with her shoulder, refusing to touch the glass with her hands, and we headed right into the rain.

"GG, does it always rain at Heathrow?" I asked remembering it always seemed to be raining when I arrived.

"Pretty much, but no one comes to London for the weather, and don't you get plenty of sunshine in California? There you are always frosting yourself with SPF 1000, and here you don't have to."

"I think it is SPF 30," I replied as we both tried to steer my wobbly luggage trolley along the crowded walkway.

In England they speak English, and so do we in the United States. But there are many times we use different words for the same thing. In America we say luggage cart or shopping cart and in England they say trolley. I always like to learn new words. When I go back home I share them with my friends.

"What a ghastly cart, Abby. It sounds like it is on its last journey. Hurry along before it explodes." I gave it a big push, but it kept screeching at us.

The trolley had a wonky wheel. Wonky is another much-used British word. It means wacky and not normal. That wheel was making a lot of noise as we were bumping along. GG loves to get attention, but not the kind made with a thumping cart, so she was walking really fast.

GG with her painstaking travel planning had spent a lot of time coordinating my arrival from California and our immediate departure to Italy. She planned our journeys like General Patton planned troop movement, and she felt it a personal failure if things did not go smoothly.

"Your clever grandmother has checked us in online; now we are off to our gate. You probably feel like a little exercise after sitting on that long flight?" We headed off toward security pushing our luggage trolley loaded with bags of travel togs and guide books and of course lots of shoes.

While we walked under the shelter that connects the terminal gates trying to stay dry, GG looked at me, and her eyebrows started to dance. First she asked, "How was your flight?" and then added, "Oh, and why you are wearing someone else's clothes?" As I said, some things never change.

My new shirt with just one sleeve might have been pushing it. I knew she was going to give me that funny look, and she did. That's why I wore it on the plane, so she would see it first thing. My Dad told me when I do things like that I am being provocative, but really I just wanted to get this conversation out of the way early.

"They're new."

GG had not had much luck in directing my wardrobe for our previous travels, and this time she did give me money but did not give me a theme. She had relied on what she called my delightful Boho Chic style, but just now she did not appear to be too pleased with the results.

GG cleared her throat. "Your Mom has good fashion sense; I was rather hoping she would help you make some choices?"

"No, these choices were all mine." Then I looked over at GG and perked up. I changed the subject. "I like your new hair cut. It's way cooler than that helmet you had last year."

GG beamed, "It is quite a lot shorter. Do you really like it?"

"Sure." I reached up and twirled a curl of hair by her ear, which made her smile. Then she snapped her teeth like she was trying to bite me. I jumped and we giggled.

GG's hair looked pretty. "How long did you have your hair that other way?"

She patted her hair and with a look of regret in her eyes told me, "I don't remember, and as you can see it is gone now." She tossed her head from side to side and added, "Very recently I have decided to start wearing hats again. You like hats, don't you?" She patted a piece of her luggage that I guess was meant to show me it was full of hats.

"Yep." I do. I like to wear hats; in fact I am known for it. I don't wear hats to hide my hair; I do it because each hat is different and I like to match the hats to the mood I am in. I have 23 hats, so there is always one that fits the day just right.

"GG, you are all dressed up. Are we going to a party?" I asked her with a grin.

"Life is a party, darling, and you must be ready for what the day might bring."

"What if the day brings a hike in the hills or a game of mini golf?" She doesn't look ready for that, I thought.

"I can promise you those are not on our agenda." She winked at me.

"How many hours is this next flight?" I was plenty tired of airports and flights.

"Less than two hours, and Florence is more than worth it. Florence is an essential city on our 21st Century Grand Tour and one of my favorite places on the planet."

"Is it a really fancy place?" Hoping it was not, but knowing my grandmother liked formal places the best.

"No, dear, not like that. It is very old and the outsides of the buildings can look really rather dull, but inside are treasures for us to discover. We will have to be great detectives like Miss Marple and Nancy Drew. You like puzzles, don't you?"

I nodded yes that I did, but I was not sure what she meant about being detectives in Florence, and my mind flashed back to Dick Tracy. Now I was suspicious. What is she up to now? Wonder if my Dad knows?

Getting on the plane took a bit of shuffling around. GG and I did not have seats together, which I knew would irritate her and that she would soon fix.

GG tried to get the attention of our flight attendant, but she kept ignoring GG and talking to the man sitting by me. I wasn't sure if GG's hair was on fire, but right now I could just about see the flames starting.

GG was clearing her throat really loud and making some funny hand gestures, but the cabin attendant just refused to look at her. GG doesn't like to be ignored when she is trying to correct a problem. Who does?

GG looked at me and with a nod softly said, "Hold on." I nodded back as if in code. Then GG pushed into the aisle and while smiling really big and fluttering her eyes she asked the man if he would switch seats with her.

He seemed a bit surprised to be interrupted and looked at the stewardess and then back again to GG. He smiled, "But of course, signora," and then said something to the flight attendant in Italian and moved to the row behind us.

I never doubted GG could fix the problem. "Abby, I think Fabio and Barbie just made a date for dinner at a posh place in Florence." Posh is another fancy English word. It means rich and snooty.

GG and I always ride in the front of planes because the seats are bigger, and GG said her backside would not fit in the little seats in the back. I don't think that is true. I think she likes to sit up front because it is easier to get on and off the plane. And we can start the vacation sooner. Hey, it works for me.

I was playing with my IPad and turned to her. "GG, do you want some gummy bears?" I had bought a big bag at the airport. She shook her head no. I leaned down to grab my sweets from my backpack and noticed GG's shoes. They were short boots with really high heels. She caught me looking and gave her ankle a couple of twists. "Aren't they fabulous? They came in blue too, and I could hardly resist getting both colors." I bet she did get them both; it is not in GG's DNA to resist shoes.

Fiddling with my IPad didn't last long, as I was beginning to fall asleep. California is eight hours behind London and nine hours behind Italy. This is because the earth turns, and that makes it different times in different places. It was, after all, a very long time since I had departed Santa Barbara. My eyeballs were still on California time.

There was a loud screechy noise, and it jolted me up. "I am Captain DePaulo. We will be landing soon. If you look out the right side of the plane you will see the magnificent Duomo of Florence. Please make sure your seatbelts are fastened for landing."

GG reached over and gave me a happy pat and pointed to the city swirling into view below the clouds. Reaching almost up to the clouds was the tall curvy red top on a huge church. Benvenuto a Firenze, our Grand Tour of Florence was about to begin.

First thing off the plane, we had to get onto a little shuttle bus and take a short ride across the tarmac to the terminal. I was just about to grab the rail when GG nudged me and handed me a wet wipe.

"Thanks, GG," then I dutifully wiped off my hands. She sure hates germs, maybe a little too much, but that rail did look kind of slimy.

The lines for Passport Control were pretty short. Our plane wasn't very large, and all the Italian people used a different entrance. This would be my first stamp from

Italy. "GG, everyone is very quiet. Are they sleepy?"

"No, sweetheart. A long time ago they had some trouble here, and some people got hurt. There is no more trouble like that now, but security is very serious here and people are always quiet in Italian airports to show they have no mischief in mind."

"Buon giorno," I said to the agent.

He looked down at me and with a smile said "Buon giorno, signorina," right back. With a clunk he stamped me in.

It did not take long to get our luggage and get out of the airport; like Santa Barbara the airport in Florence is not at all large. We headed to a car that was waiting near the airport entry. The driver had a sign with our name.

Soon we were bouncing along in the back seat heading to the hotel. I looked out the car windows for my first look at Florence, and it looked very different from London or Santa Barbara. Everything looked old and slightly dusty, rather like a toy that had been left out in a sand box.

"What do you think? How do you like it?" asked GG. I felt like she was rushing me for an opinion, but I could tell by her happy voice that she was excited to be here. I did not want to tell her I thought it looked kind of dirty and old.

Instead, I nodded my head and said, "Looks different." GG liked that answer. Sometimes it is easier to give grownups the answers they want and save our opinions for ourselves, but mostly in our family kids' opinions count. So I felt a little like I was cheating GG out of the truth, but I really wasn't yet sure what I thought of this place.

"Well put, it is very different here. And there are so many hidden treasurers to find."

"Miss Marple and Nancy Drew, that's us."

"I do so want you to love it as I do. Starting with our hotel, where they will take very good care of us."

"Do they have a pool? I brought my swimming suit and goggles." GG looked surprised at the question.

"No, no one comes to Florence to swim," said GG. "And we won't have time for that. Anyway, don't you have lots of time to swim at home? We want to do things you don't get to do in California." It made me wonder what we were actually going to be doing in this dusty town, but I knew GG would have a game plan. She always did.

Just as we parked and stepped out of the car, a tubby little man came rushing up to us. "Buon giorno, signora." He twirled on his heels to look at me. With a shake of his head he put his hands on his cheeks and declared, "Bellissimo!"

GG was beaming with pride while he was bouncing with excitement. He really seemed pleased to see us. "I am Massimo and you must be Abigaile? Your grandmother has been coming to Florence for many years, and each time she tells us she is so looking forward to the time she can share our city with her granddaughter. This is a most happy occasion for us all. I do hope your journey was a pleasant one? Now let me show you to your suite."

I didn't mean to be disrespectful, but couldn't help myself and started to giggle. Massimo made me think of a big balloon that was losing air fast. I whispered, "He is funny, he talks very fast, and he never once took a breath, not once."

"Yes, sweetie, that is the Italian way. They are very enthusiastic in conversation."

Before our trips GG always asks me to learn to speak a

few words in the language of the country we are going to visit. Hello, thank you, and toilet she says are always useful. In other countries they say toilet and not bathroom, powder room, or restroom. If you say those words they will not know where you want to go.

Buon giorno means hello, but I did not know what bellissima meant, though I could tell it was something good. Later GG told me that it means extra beautiful. I don't think I have ever been called extra beautiful before in any language.

Massimo then said to GG, "Signora, you too bellissima." GG likes to be flattered. My Dad told me she is like that because Grandpa Ted was always telling her she was beautiful, and now that he is gone she misses hearing that. I always tell her she is pretty because she is and because it makes her smile real big when I say it. Massimo had her beaming with his compliment.

Then she told Massimo she was going to be wearing hats, and that made him shake his head in disapproval. He told her he liked her new coiffeur. Which I guess means hairdo if you are in a fancy hotel.

Our room at the Grand Hotel was fancy. GG likes a lot of space and I am used to her extravagance, but this room was even more so than usual. I headed to an open window that was really the doors to a small balcony.

"Good call, GG, this is a great perch." I went right out on it and looked at the Arno River that runs by the side of the hotel. There were loads of people walking by.

"GG, where is everyone going?"

"This is Italy." She flung her arms wide, clearly pleased with my first reaction. "People just stroll around. Presenting the

'Bella Figura,' it is called. Looking your best." GG stood tall and raised one arm high above her head.

I wonder if those were two more Italian words I need to remember, but I didn't ask. "Abby, these walks are like going to the mall at home, but much dressier. It is where people meet and visit with their friends and sometimes make new ones."

GG quickly offered a handful of money to the departing Massimo. This was a gratuity. GG explained to me it is a special way to say thank you when someone has been helpful.

"GG, my Mom told me you are rich, but you are always giving money away. You give money to people that help us and even to strangers. I hope you have enough left?"

"I hope so too." She giggled. "But I don't like tightwads. Anyway, your Grandfather taught me it is not how much you spend that matters, it is how much you earn. I save my worries for that and have fun with the spending part."

I returned to the window when I saw three brightly colored motorbikes zip by. "Yes," I said while doing a little air pump. "Oh boy, that looks like fun. GG, look, those motorcycles; can we take a ride?" I was pointing my fingers rapidly toward the street.

"Vespas."

"I don't know what they are called, but I want to ride one please?" I bounced as I pleaded, thinking it looked like so much fun, and knowing GG was a big softie and usually let me do what I wanted. I could tell I was old enough to ride, as I had even seen small children clinging to the backs of grownups as they zoomed by with their hair flying. One even had a little brown dog in a basket.

"We are going to be awfully busy." I could see my

Grandmother was horrified at the very idea of me riding on one of those.

Maybe she is too old, I thought, though I did not say so since age talk makes her grumpy. "I don't think we will be able to do that on this visit." Hum? No swimming and no scooters. When is the fun going to begin, I thought. "Well, GG, you did buy me that cool scooter to ride around your island."

GG ignored that, and then said a very odd thing. "You don't have a tattoo, do you?"

Ok, that one was out there even for GG. "Gosh no, I am not even allowed to have pierced ears yet." She sure gets wild ideas sometimes. "Why do you want to know that?"

"People who like motorcycles often like tattoos, and I don't want you to like them."

"No problem there. Remember, Wheels likes motorcycles and he doesn't have a tattoo."

Now she was making a funny face. "Ah, GG are you ok? You have kind of a scrunched up look."

"It's nothing much, my feet are just a bit sore after the long day, that is all."

"Maybe you should not wear those high heels at your age," I said. I knew mentioning age would make her forget about the motorcycles. It sure worked. She looked like she ate a gold fish.

GG cleared her throat. "For safety and comfort I want to list a few rules for our stay here."

GG makes lists of everything. She has told me "lists are an essential aid to a tidy mind and orderly life." I like lists too; keeps obligations and expectations nice and clear. "List away."

My Dad calls GG the List Queen, which she thinks is a compliment. She makes the rules and we always break them, but she really likes to make them anyway.

"First we will not be riding scooters, you cannot wear clothes with only one sleeve, and you won't mention my age for any reason. Agreed?" That sounded pretty easy, so I just nodded as I closed the balcony door.

GG stood in the middle of the room and turned all the way around. "Oh no! Abby, one of our bags is missing, my big designer bag that has the extra band on the side. You remember it, don't you?" I nodded yes.

Isn't that the one they made you pay extra for because it was too heavy?"

Her eyes flared. "It certainly was. First they charge us extra, and now they don't even get it to Florence."

I quickly did another glance around the room and even peeked under the beds. Yep it was not here.

"Well, at least my shoe bag made it. Remind me to have Massimo call the airline." Not willing to spend any additional precious time on lost luggage, GG reached into one of her pieces of designer luggage that had make it and retrieved a stack of maps and guidebooks and handed the lump to me. "Take a look at these beauties; I have spent years getting just the right collection together."

GG always gets carried away with maps and guidebooks. Her office in London even has map wallpaper. Ever since she discovered Amazon on the net she was constantly sending me map things. She also sent a globe that lights up and a floor puzzle map of the world for Penny.

Every time the UPS truck rumbles into our cul de sac in

Santa Barbara, Daddy and I look at each other and try to guess which country GG was on about this time.

My lips were curled in a snarl as I continued to eye the mound. I wanted to make it clear my grandmothers' plan did not include carrying this heavy stuff around the city. "Haven't you been here a lot of times, GG? Do we need to lug all of this heavy stuff with us?" I dreaded that thought. I don't like to carry anything when I walk around looking at things.

"Yes, I mean no. Yes, I have been here many times, and no, we don't have to take these things. I just thought you might want to check out where we are and where we are going. I even have a map for the wall."

With excitement GG bounded across the room and jerked up a duffle bag that had been placed on the floor. She plopped it on the bed and plunged in elbow deep. She rustled around, then retrieved a large map, which she unfurled with a flourish. "Ta-da." She patted the bag and dove in again, and this time she produced a roll of Scotch tape with which to hang the map on the back of the door.

She thinks of everything.

"Help me over here, sweetie." GG flipped open the large map. It seemed to be refusing to go flat. "Take one side." GG fought wildly with the curling edges. It just did not want to open out, so we ended up dancing around and getting the giggles as we tried to hang it evenly. Finally, completed but defeated the map stretched across the back of the large door, but when we stood back to admire our efforts, it was all droopy on one side. We looked at each other and GG sighed. "It's an immutable law; maps refuse to go flat, refold, or hang straight. That will just have to do." She grabbed a Sharpie from a side pouch and made a large X. "We are here. The Grand Excelsior Hotel."

She does try to make things fun, but I groaned silently, closed my eyes, and exhaled after again eyeing the bulky stack she was now shuffling on her lap as she sat in the desk chair.

"This stuff is great, but after two days I am kind of sick of my backpack."

"I think that it would be a shame not to take a few. I have always loved maps, and they keep you from getting lost."

"No problem there, GG, I have a map app on my phone," I proudly told her, hoping to educate her to an easier, lightweight option.

"No. No, our theme is antiquities and all those electronics will interfere. I must ask you to turn off all gadgets and leave them in the suite."

"Ok I got it, another one for the list of rules."

GG sure is different from my Mom, who never goes anywhere without her cell phone, not even the dinner table. Penny and I often eat dinner while watching our Mom nibbling her food while texting or talking on the phone or reading her emails on her IPad.

Penny doesn't mind. She's gabby and doesn't seem to notice if no one is listening, but I do and wish my Mom would talk to us at dinner, but I guess she is busy. My Mom calls it multi-tasking, but it is not fair because if a kid tried that they would be called rude.

GG gave a big yawn. "I am feeling a wee bit tired. I think I will just kick back here for a moment." She fell back and stretched out as far as she could on the fluffy bed. "How gorgeous, a lavender scented down cloud," she murmured as she kicked off her shoes and wiggled deep into the crisp linen. The crystal lights twinkling on the Venetian crystal high above seemed to hypnotize her and she was soon lulled to sleep. I decided to go back out on our little balcony, but first I washed up and changed into some fresh clothes.

I was not out there very long when I looked directly below the terrace and saw Fabio from the plane. He was shouting at a short mean-faced man who stomped his foot. They were so heated I thought someone was going to get punched. I was trying hard to hear what they were saying, but the noise from the cars and the Vespas made it difficult, and then I realized they were speaking in Italian.

"Oh, did I nap long?" GG sputtered. She sat up with a start as I walked back through the glass doors. GG was shaking her head trying to wake up while pulling a creased guidebook from beneath her.

"GG, guess who I saw on the street below us?" GG grabbed me and pulled me into her cloud of covers. She gave me a big hug, still warm from her rest.

"I don't know, who? Katy Perry, the Pope?" she replied with a groggy giggle.

"No, I saw that Fabio man you took the seat from on the plane."

"I didn't take it, dear, he gave it to me."

"Sure, GG, whatever, but he was talking out there to a fat, mean-looking guy," I said while pointing out the window. "I could not understand them. I think they were speaking Italian."

"Of course they were."

"You could see our plane man was not happy and he was

waving his arms around like he was giving orders or telling him off." I demonstrated the arm waving.

"Waving your arms about in Italy does not mean you are unhappy. That is how most Italians speak. It shows passion and enthusiasm."

"He looked mad to me, and what was he doing here?"

"Florence is not big; at least in the center where we are; it is not uncommon to run into people you have seen in other places. It makes you feel right at home here to see people you know."

GG was now sitting up in her bed. She wiggled her toes. "These tootsies really enjoyed that rest," then she kicked off the duvet. "Now what are your thoughts about dinner?"

"I'm hungry. How about pizza?"

"No, we will save those for lunches." She rocked me side to side, and we started to giggle.

"Tonight we dine. Oh and let's dress up a little, ok?" she urged as she swung her legs out and gave her head a good shake. She pushed me out of the bed.

"I am dressed up. I washed my face and put this on while you were sleeping. You bought this too, and it cost a lot." I had hoped the mention of the price tag would garner my grandmother's approval. It didn't work. She raised her eyebrows really high and said, "I never bought you anything that color in my life. In fact, I have never seen that particular color in all my 55 years of life."

"Fifty-five? GG, I am pretty sure my Dad said you were sixty something?" Normally, as I said, I do not mention age to her, but I was kind of confused that my Dad did not know how old his Mom is. Or was it she who didn't know?

"What did I say about that? Remember the rules?" GG huffed, acting like my Dad had betrayed her.

Plop goes the birthday cake. Poor GG, I will just have to cheer her up. "Oh sure, sorry. I meant I bought it for the trip with the money you sent to me. You don't seem to like any of my new clothes."

GG was horrified that she might have hurt my feelings and quickly reached out and hugged me again. "Of course I do. You always look cute."

Ok, that worked, I thought. Now I knew I could wear anything I wanted. Grown-ups always think they are the only clever ones. They think they can trick us into doing what they want, and often they can. But we kids are pretty resourceful too.

"Oh, darling, you know how much I like to show you off to all of my friends. Now would I do that if I didn't like your clothes? No, we just need to coordinate a bit."

I know what coordinate means, but I wondered what she was up to. "What does that mean?" I asked her suspiciously, but knowing I had won this round.

"Share ideas and suggestions. Like when you suggested I not wear high heels. Well, that was a good idea, and my feet will feel better tomorrow if I take your advice. Thank you for suggesting that. So see, we are helping each other. Now please take that ghastly color off and try again."

Then, with great daring, I answered GG back, "Ok, I will, if you won't wear those high heels to dinner. They will hurt your feet and just make you feel bad."

GG tilted her head with a curious smile and feeling slightly suspicious I had out-maneuvered her. She replied, "You are a clever girl. Ok, no heels tonight. Now please get changed so we can go."

I jumped up. "I'm on it," I said and returned in a jiffy.

"They eat later here, so we are a little early by Italian standards, but I am starving. As they say in Italy, 'Fame de lupo!' Hungry as a wolf."

I made a wolf howl, "Iooooah," to indicate I agreed.

"This is a surprise. You told me Buco Maria was your favorite place, so I was certain it would be all fancy-pants, but now we are walking down rock stairs into what looks like a cave."

"It's a cellar, and it is huge. A whole series of small, connected underground rooms." And just then the wonderful aromas of garlic and grilled foods enclosed us. "Just take a whiff. The fancy part is the treat for your taste buds. They will be in heaven." We were soon seated in the front room. The table was small and covered with a crisp white cloth. There was a drippy red candle stuck in a bottle and on the table were bread sticks, olives, and chunks of Parmesan cheese. I was hungry, so I started to nibble right away. The ceilings were low, and the walls looked like a cave. It felt warm and cozy; I could see why GG liked the place.

A tiny lady with really dark hair hurried over to us. "Welcome back, GG," she said as she did a light kiss on each side of GG's face. "We have missed you, and this must be your lovely granddaughter." Turning to me she leaned down and looked right in my eyes. "Oh yes, we have seen many photos of you and have been anxiously awaiting your first visit to Florence." I guess GG does like to brag about me to her friends. Seems like everyone in Florence was waiting for my visit.

GG told me that Maria was the owner, and they had known each other for many years. Maria was tiny, but I looked at her feet, and she was wearing the tallest shoes I have ever seen. I was thinking those two probably go shoe shopping together.

"Oh Signora Gable, you have changed your hair style; it is so smart and youthful." She squinted as she looked at GG's feet. "Ah, new flat shoes. You Americans are so sensible."

She laughed as she moved away to a nearby table. GG hates flat shoes. She called them boring old lady shoes and after Maria mentioned them I felt kind of bad I had tricked her into wearing them to dinner.

"Sensible! How insulting," GG snorted. "I think my steak was overcooked the last time I was here."

"Does that mean I should not order the steak?" and what does that have to do with her shoes, I thought?

"Oh, never mind about that. Let's order." GG snatched up the menu. And took a gulp of her drink.

Yum. The dinner was delicious. I had grilled chicken with spaghetti. It doesn't sound special, but they way they fixed it was so good I ate every bite and washed it down with an orange soda as GG continued to sell Florence.

"Abby, this city is historic." She dipped her roll in a small saucer of olive oil and herbs, then took a quick nibble. "Some of the world's most important discoveries, inventions, and thinking came from right here. And I can't wait to show you."

"Thinking?" How is she going to show me that I thought as I reached for another bread stick.

GG signaled the waiter for the bill. "Are you ready?"

I nodded, gave my mouth a final wipe with the napkin, and gave a playful salute.

When we emerged from the cellar it was dark. There were still many people on the street and plenty of taxis waiting near the door, but GG said, "Let's walk back and enjoy the nice, balmy weather."

Walking sounded good to me. My tummy was stuffed, so I nodded my head in agreement and grabbed GG's hand.

"It is dark, but don't be concerned; with common sense and a few precautions this area of Florence is very safe well into the night." She squeezed my hand as we passed by groups of people just standing around or leaning on Vespas.

Wandering through the narrow, well-lit streets brought back many wonderful memories for GG and she was telling me all about the many times she and Grandpa Ted had taken this same walk, when suddenly I squealed and pointed toward a garbage bin.

"Look. GG, a kitten, let's try to pet her!" I headed over and bent down, trying to coax the scraggly kitty into my arms.

"Careful, Abby, the cats in Italy are not as friendly as the ones at home. These cats can be very hungry and dirty," she cautioned, trying to discourage me. I half expected her to get a wet wipe out and start after the kitty.

"Let me try. I think it's hungry. I wish I had saved some of my dinner." The curious kitten now stopped and came closer. As I extended my hands it softly meowed. I think she smelled some chicken and started to lick my finger with her tiny, coarse tongue. GG looked horrified and curled her lips, but didn't say anything.

Just then a car noisily turned the nearby corner, and the frightened kitten took off. In a flash the kitty darted through the gates of an enormous villa. Just as quickly, I followed and GG did too. It was very dark inside, and the cavernous grounds quickly enclosed us.

"Abby, Abby darling, where are you? We are not supposed to be in here," whispered GG as we stumbled along a heavily graveled courtyard.

I rustled through the bushes and finally pulled the tiny cat into my arms. "I got her GG, I got her!"

"It is so dark in here. Are you sure you are not petting a rat or old house slipper?"

"No, GG she is not a rat or slipper, she is so sweet."

"Ok, but now let's try to find our way out of here before we are discovered." It was very dark now, and GG did not seem to know which way to go. She reached out and grabbed the shoulder of my sweater and we staggered along in the deep, loose stones going slowly in what we hoped was the direction of the gate. The crunching of the gravel beneath our feet seemed to loudly echo off the high stone walls, and GG whispered she was worried we might be heard.

We rounded a thicket of big, sticky shrubbery and saw the lit interior of one of the rooms in the big house. "Wow."

GG stopped abruptly and said with pride, "See what I told you about hidden treasures? We have found one." The room was enormous and had elegant furniture with heavy fabric in blue and gold. There was a huge chandelier in the middle, and it lit the whole room in a twinkly magical light.

"Just call me Nancy," I added happily while stroking the scrawny cat.

Looking into the villa, GG whispered, "Ah, and look at that painting." Hanging above a massive stone fireplace was an enormous oil painting.

"Naked babies flying above a bed?" I said.

"It is a masterpiece." GG was now practically swooning.

Standing right in front and gazing up at the painting was the man from the plane. "GG, it's him."

"It certainly is. Hello Fabio, this grand villa must be his home."

Another man suddenly came into view. A short and menacing looking man who handed the handsome man a long tube. "That's him, GG, that's him, the man from the sidewalk today."

"Oh my, he is a troll." Her spell was broken.

"You speak Italian; what are they shouting about now?"

"My Italian is a bit rusty, and I cannot really hear them from here." GG had previously told me that it is not easy to learn a new language when you are an adult. She said I should study Spanish and French while I am young. I started to move toward the window when GG grabbed me and pulled me back.

"Hold on, honey." GG was now cautious. Her body went quite stiff with concern. In that single moment, I dropped the squirming kitten and bent over to retrieve it. Suddenly, there was what sounded like a muffled pop. GG gasped, I nearly cried out with surprise, but stopped myself just in time. GG thrust her hands out in the darkness to calm me. I did not know if she was trying to assure me or keep me still, but I was glad she was there. It all happened very quickly, then everything seemed to stop. I too went quite stiff with worry.

Fabio was now standing alone. The dark burly man was now no longer visible. We stayed frozen in the dark as he still calmly enjoyed the painting.

Next he removed the painting from the wall and began quickly detaching it from the frame. Then he rolled the canvas in a tight cylinder and unrolled the tube the brutish man had given him. He placed in the frame a picture that seemed identical to the one he had removed. It made no sense.

"Abby, I think that beautiful painting is being stolen."

"But how can he steal his own painting? Maybe he has two."

"It is confusing, but—" GG abruptly stopped talking.

The man had stepped though the villa doors and with elaborate casualness walked right toward us.

"Drop," GG said softly. And we both hit the gravel. He closely brushed past our hiding place and went out the still open iron gates.

We had been too frightened to speak. I had held my breath. I had instinctively remained very still and did not make a sound, but I wanted to howl. My shins were hurt as I had scraped them on the stones. Now it felt dark and spooky.

At just this time the kitten let out a high-pitched squeal and darted from my grasp, then bounded off toward the still slightly opened gate. The man paused and looked in our direction, but the darkness was too thick and we were not seen.

GG started moving slowly. I have a pretty good sense of direction and was sure she was going the wrong way. I took her hand and tugged it in another direction and without a word she followed me. I proceeded slowly and as soundlessly as possible through the shadows and heavy foliage as we crept nearer the exit. We lingered in the shadows, hoping to remain hidden, but this was tricky, as we needed to get out of there.

I hadn't noticed it earlier, but in the glow of a yellow light attached outside the villa wall I was able to see the faint outline of a nearby car. Fabio walked to the front of the car and leaned toward the side window. He passed the rolled-up painting to the driver and seemed to be speaking, though we could not hear what he said. It was too dark for us to really see who might be in the shadowy interior of the car, as the engine started and slowly the car pulled away from the curb.

GG and I stayed hidden, but I was really scared now. My full tummy was churning. I was holding my breath and was sure we would be seen, but the man calmly walked back through the gates brushing terribly near us before he returned to the interior of the house.

Yikes! I was feeling anything but calm. My heart was galloping. "Go." GG took my hand and pulled me quickly through the bushes and out the gate to safety just before we heard the rusty lock thud shut behind us.

"Phew. We made it," I said. GG let out her breath and rested her hand on my shoulder. She kissed me on the top of my head and whispered, "We're ok." But the kitten was gone.

GG did not want to frighten me, but she did. "Abby, we must tell the police what we have seen."

"What have we seen, GG?" I still wasn't sure.

"I am not entirely certain what we have seen either, but if

my first impression is correct, I feel certain something is very wrong. Give me your phone."

"Sorry, but you told me I was not to carry it with me; it was one of the rules." I held my palms up as if to demonstrate the missing phone.

"Yes, yes the rules. I did, and thank you for remembering." I was feeling shaky now. I could tell from her voice GG was too.

"Darling, don't worry. There is a police station near the piazza in front of our hotel. We will go there at once and tell them what just happened."

I was worried. I had begun nervously gnawing on my bottom lip and fidgeting with the hem of my jacket. It is very disturbing when grownups get worried. They are always working hard to make us feel safe, but when grownups don't feel safe it is really quite scary.

The Questura, which is an Italian police station, was about ten minutes away, and I bet GG was glad now she was in boring old lady flat shoes, because she was practically running to get us there.

The building was huge and shadowy and kind of sinister in the dark. There were quiet men with guns standing outside. They did not look like policemen, more like people in a parade all dressed up, but with big guns. GG said they were called the Carabinieri, and they were known for always being handsome and well dressed.

It felt a lot better inside, where it was bright and noisy. We could hear people shouting and doors banging. But the people at the reception desk were calm and friendly. It smelled like Starbucks.

"Signora," they said to GG as we stood in front of the high reception desk. "Please calm yourself." GG nodded while drawing deep, gasping breaths. She seemed to be trying to show a certain degree of lucidity, but she could only manage to babble. I nodded rapidly in a show of support, as my heart was still pounding from the run and I couldn't really speak.

"You say there may have been a murder and possibly the theft of a painting just tonight? And you and your granddaughter witnessed this and you know who the thief and murderer is?"

He turned to the man standing next to him and said, "How very fortunate, it seems they have done our work for us." Then they chortled and I thought GG would get mad, but instead, still excited and somewhat breathless, she said, "I know this all sounds a bit fantastic, but I assure you I am not making this up."

"She is telling you the truth," I said.

"Thank you, dear. I am telling the truth." GG had turned to look at me, but now looked back at the two officers. "I told you we were coming from dinner." I was nodding with enthusiastic support so they would believe her. The Carabinieri continued listening to GG in a very relaxed manner.

"And where was this meal?" one of the officers inquired.

"Buco Maria," I replied. I was smiling, remembering our tasty dinner.

He smiled back at me and said, "Of course, one of our city's finest." He turned to GG. "And did you have an excellent dinner?

"Yes, absolutely marvelous, but we are not here to discuss food. There has been a crime."

"It was real scary," I added.

"Signora, you say you were trespassing on the grounds of the Villa Flurio when you happen to see all of this in the dark?"

"Just like Miss Marple," I added, again trying to be helpful.

"Ahh yes, signora, the famous Meese Marple. And this is how you see yourself, perhaps?" he asked her with no small amount of sarcasm in his voice.

"I know what you are implying and I don't like it, and we were not exactly trespassing."

"We followed a cat inside," I said.

"A cat? Not a pink elephant or perhaps and a polar bear? Though none have been seen in this area for quite some time," said one of the officers as he winked at me.

Huh? What did he mean by polar bears and elephants? This was all getting pretty weird.

"All right, very amusing young man, but I am not at all imagining things." GG was cross now. I was thinking her hair was just about to ignite.

"We will be happy to take your report, signora, and add it to the others."

"You remember me?" asked a startled GG.

"Oh yes, a visit from Meese Marple is not to be forgotten. Now please, could we have the correct spelling of your surname?"

It was boring and took a while, but after finishing the paperwork we finally made it back to our hotel. We were dog-tired from our busy day, and after we washed our faces and brushed our teeth we fell into our big, comfy beds.

"GG, this bed feels so good." I curled in a ball and tucked the duvet tightly under my chin. "Do you think they believed us?"

"They would be foolish not to." GG rolled side to side, positioning herself in the bed. She said she wanted to enjoy every inch possible of the heavenly fabrics. Then she loudly sighed, "It was a marvelous first day in Florence together. And I don't care if those policemen did not believe us; we did the right thing by reporting the crime. Now I am going to try to dream in Italian tonight. Buona notte."

Our brief, cozy slumber was abruptly halted. "Poliza! Signora, please open this door. Subito!" GG and I bolted upright in our beds to thunderous pounding on our door and much shouting and commotion in the hallway. Then without delay, the door flew open and we were faced with a well-dressed wall of Carabinieri whose eyes softened as they took in the opulence of the suite. GG glared at Massimo as he shrugged sheepishly and held out the key.

"GG, what is happening?"

"Yes, gentlemen, what is happening? Is the hotel on fire?" GG asked with alarm. I was trying to shake my head awake, but did not want to relinquish my cozy bed.

"Signora, we must ask you to come with us at once," demanded one of the tall men.

"Ok," said a disoriented GG. "If you will give me time to dress I would be hap-"

"No, signora, you must come now." GG looked at me and shrugged.

Dressed in a voluminous red and gold caftan, very high heels, and in a cloud of perfume GG emerged from our suite with me right behind her. "GG, you look kind of fancy. Are we supposed to get dressed up?" I was wearing a soft warm-up suit and still felt pretty cozy.

"No, sweetie, but having only slept a few winks I was feeling in every way I might needed a boost." It wasn't such a good plan. Her tall shoes proved very difficult in the dark as she stumbled toward the station across the piazza of cobblestones. On my feet I had pink Uggs, and they felt great. Would she ever learn?

Entering the building it was not like before. Now it was very quiet. A big man with a smile soon greeted us, "Signora Gable, I am Marshal Ridormi, commanding officer of this station."

GG turned to me, smiled, and whispered, "Hercules". She had just named him. My Dad is a big guy, but this guy was much bigger, so I guess the name fit him pretty well. He led us past the front reception area we had been to earlier and into the inner sanctum of the facility.

This ancient, converted monastery with its high ceilings and displaying church paintings on the walls was juxtaposed against computers, video monitors, and gadgets that made me feel as if we had been summoned to the command center for the Space Station. I was still trying to wake up, but this was all looking very strange.

"Please sit down," he said as he pointed his big arm toward two empty wooden chairs."

GG had a big smile on her face, and I knew she thought the marshal was handsome. He looked like a movie star. "I apologize for not being here to take your statement earlier."

"It is probably not correct to have the child with you while we have our discussion," he offered politely. I did not want to have to wait out front by myself so I said, "Oh that is ok, and I have been to the police station with her lots of times."

"Can this be true? Please tell me about this, signorina? And Paolo, please open that window slightly," commanded the marshal.

Good idea, I thought. GG's perfume was filling up the little room. When he said that she looked a bit embarrassed, though not for long.

"Please then, proceed."

"Once we were questioned after a man with a cane fell at Pirates of the Caribbean," I answered.

"You fought pirates in the Caribbeano?" quizzed the startled marshal whose eyes were now quite large.

"No, we were on the Pirates of the Caribbean," I said.

"Wait," GG interrupted. "You will not question her, I will tell you if you must know. A horrible little man patted me in an inappropriate way, so I pushed him in the water."

"He really was horrible, so she threw his cane in too. It hit his head."

"How was I to know he couldn't swim?" GG looked at me, and we nodded in agreement.

"Well, signora, in Italy, a little pat would not have been

seen as a big crime, but to drown someone is frowned upon."

"He started it," I said. GG sat tall and I did too.

"What other police adventures have you two had, may I ask?" This time he asked this with what I was certain was a slight smirk, and I knew GG would not like that.

"I don't recall any others," replied GG.

"Oh, I do. Remember in London?" I offered, hoping to get this over soon and get back to bed.

"Darling, try not to increase my stress by helping. But yes, yes, there was a slight misunderstanding at the park."

"Please proceed, tell me about this misunderstanding, signora," the marshal queried while making notes.

"It was nothing, really."

I jumped back into the conversation. "We were victims of a gang of purse snatchers. We defended ourselves."

"And the police?" again asked the marshal.

"GG clobbered the kid."

"What kid, ah child?" asked the marshal. "You hurt a child?" The marshal's eyes looked serious as he looked at GG.

"The purse snatchers were two boys, and they were hitting us," I said.

GG stuttered, "It was self-defense. I was just trying to get my bag back from the little scamps." She was really trying to downplay things.

"The police came and GG was still so mad she was yelling at the policeman, and I was wet and mucky from the duck pond and…" The Marshal starred at us with a look of bewilderment.

GG interrupted me now. "It was a bit chaotic, but the misunderstanding was all sorted out. Eventually."

"It took forever, GG, remember how angry you were and that policeman said he was going to have you retrained."

"Restrained, sweetie, and happily it never came to that."

"It was a misunderstanding," I said. GG nodded at me again.

"Yes, that is exactly what it was. Now can we please return to the reason you woke us in the middle of the night and dragged us over here?"

"Signora please, I must protest. No one dragged, you did they? There was no hint of brutality, and I must insist you do not make such a claim."

"Brutality? No, nothing like that." GG and I shook our heads.

"I didn't mean actually dragged," said my grandmother in a very cranky voice. "We are here now; what do you want us for?"

The marshal ignored her question and her crabby tone. "Tell me, please, about your visit to Villa Florio last night," he asked as he stretched out and leaned back in his big chair to listen.

I wanted to stay awake and support GG, but I kept closing my eyes. Finally I slumped forward with my head leaning on the edge of the marshal's large desk. I was just barely awake.

While I was lolling in the chair, GG spent more than twenty minutes trying to explain fully what we had seen and done.

"The Villa Flurio is one of the most famous in Florence. The art collection inside is one of our city's finest. We understand some paintings have recently been sold. We are, however, curious about your entrance to the villa?"

"I stirred in my chair and said, "It was the kitten," then closed my eyes again.

The marshal ignored me and said to GG, "The wife of Count Lamberti, the owner, has been ill and is being treated in Rome, and it had been our understanding the villa was not occupied at this time. The count is known to return for brief visits, but no one answers at the villa tonight. Perhaps he departed quickly?"

GG perked up. She was pleased that the police had followed up on their report.

"Just two more questions, signora. Can you possibly identify the brutish-looking man if we show you some photographs? And can you describe the painting?"

GG raised her hand to her face to stifle a yawn. "Impossible, I am sorry, but I am too tired to identify even my own son in a photograph." GG, too exhausted to recall much and having difficulty giving an accurate description from her memory, sighed and relayed what I had said in the villa courtyard: "Oh, a painting of a lot of naked babies flying around."

To this, the face of the marshal dropped in disappointment. Like most Florentines, he was very proud of the city's art treasures and did not like to hear them dismissed in this manner. I didn't blame GG though; it had been a very long day.

"Signora, did you see what happened after you saw the two men?" asked the marshal as he read the description from his notes.

"No. I thought I heard a shot, but did not actually see the gun. It was pretty confusing. Did you check out the villa?"

"We are not at liberty to discuss the details of the investigation with you, Miss Marple," he said with a smile. Apparently, he was reading the name from the notes the conscientious officer had made earlier in the evening. I was awake now, but just barely.

"Please, marshal, we are exhausted. Let us return to our hotel."

"Yes, of course, senora. Here is my card if you think of anything thing else. I will ask Officer Scotti to assist you across the square," graciously offered the marshal as he stood, signaling the end of our meeting.

GG pushed herself up out of the chair as the officer reached down and picked me up. I was still groggy and was happy not to walk. He carried me from the station and across the piazza, while slowly lagging behind us, GG in her very high heels hobbled and wobbled unaided across the treacherous stones. I was really tired, but I felt sorry for her feet.

"Buon giorno, mi cara. Are you ready to conquer Florence?"

"Yes, and breakfast too, I am starving." The room service waiter had just delivered orange juice, coffee, and pastry. I wanted to eat fast and get out of the room quickly before GG remembered the maps and guidebooks.

When we finished eating, GG eyed me top to toe. Apparently my outfit for the day met with her approval. No offending colors or missing sleeves, she gave me a quick nod and said, "Well done." Then she grabbed a big red hat, planted it on her head, raised her hand in a salute, and declared, "Andiamo, off we go."

Walking out of the hotel lobby we passed massive marble columns and seriously fancy-looking furniture. No one was sitting on the couches, and I bet I know why. They looked uncomfortable. We made a quick stop at the front desk, where we saw Massimo.

"Any word on our missing bag?"

"No, signora, they tell me it never arrived in Italy."

"Oh Abby, my favorite bag is probably gone forever."

GG was really annoyed, but she refused to let it ruin our day, and nudged me on through the lobby toward the hotel entrance. I quickly warmed when we were hit with a blast of hot air as we stepped out the doors and onto the vast stone piazza. We were greeted with harsh sunlight, a rush of traffic, and blaring horns.

"Ah, the city feels and sounds just as it should," declared GG as she inhaled expansively.

"What does that mean?"

"Each city has its own sounds, smells, and feel. I want you to pay attention to that and let me know if you agree." This baffled me. GG never liked conversations about poo or bad smells. Any talk like that was usually guaranteed to make her quite cross.

"It smells ok to me, GG, but I'll let you know."

GG was excited. "First thing we will walk down the river and just get a feel for this splendid city. You must ask me any questions that pop into your head. I want you to love

Florence as I do," she said with a flourish of her hand as she pointed our way to the city around us. GG loved this place, and it showed in her energetic stride.

I thought I would certainly have to love it a lot to love it as much as she does, but so far it looked okay. There were many people, Vespas, and cars going by in every direction.

"It might be a little difficult to get into some churches or museums. Just about everything in Italy has annoying hours. They take a long break right in the middle of the day, where everything just stops. We will have to make an effort to see things, but it is worthwhile."

"Some of these places look a little gloomy and really old," I said as I looked over at the stained grey walls.

"Remember, in Italy much of the beauty is hidden like a puzzle or secret to be discovered..."

I interrupted her and pinched my nose as I jumped backwards. "Why is there so much dog poop on the sidewalks and streets? Don't people pooper scoop here?"

GG halted abruptly. "What??" She looked at me with a frown and then down on the sidewalk at the pile of poo. "What kind of question is that?" she asked in a short-tempered way.

I gave a shrug. "You said I could ask you anything, and you told me to pay attention to smells." I had rather wondered why she had mentioned smells before. Now she is cross that I said something. Grownups can be confusing.

"Yes, so I did," GG replied defensively while still frowning. "But I meant ask me anything about Florence, about history and art and the architecture, not about the poo left by thoughtless dog owners."

"Well, it is actually left by the dogs." Yeah, I know I was being a bit sarcastic, which I am not allowed to do, but she wants smells, I will give her smells.

"Ok, one more thing on that list we discussed earlier, no mention of animal excrement of any kind," GG said quickly trying to end our conversation.

"Is that any kind of animal or any kind of excrement?" I was probably pushing it and being provocative, but it just seemed funny. Oh no, now I was about to get the giggles. Just as I thought GG might get very cross with this conversation she burst out laughing.

"You are winding me up, aren't you?" I nodded yes. "Enough of that, we have Florence to explore."

Dining al fresco is what the Italians call eating outside in the cool, fresh air. We were sitting in a big patio called a piazza, which GG told me is one of her favorite activities in Florence. How can sitting be an activity I wondered?

There was a parade of people going by. Everyone seemed to be having fun, except the ones lugging big heavy bags. I was really glad I had convinced GG to leave our maps and guide books in the room.

It looked like a forest of umbrellas around us. Little clumps in bright colors with Pepsi and Fanta written on them. These shaded the small tables of the cafes that went around the sides of the square. GG told me which restaurant she liked best. We went up to the door, which was actually an opening in the ornamental shrubbery. A man was standing there and smiled at GG like he knew her. She gave the man a handful of money, which made him smile even bigger, and then he led us right to the table she pointed to.

It was an almost perfect day, sunny with just a little breeze. The tables had red clamps in the shape of birds on the side to hold the tablecloths from blowing up in the wind. GG took off her hat and as usual I could hear her kick her tight shoes off under our wobbly wooden table. I looked at her, and she just shrugged back at me.

In this big area called the Piazza della Signoria there were some gigantic statues. Some were people on horses or fighting or part man, part animal. One was a large fountain, but it had no water.

"Honey, these statues are famous and don't always make sense, but for now just understand, art is just one person's idea. Remember in Los Angeles when we saw that Picasso painting of the woman with three eyes?"

"Sure, ok. Can I please have another Pepsi?" GG quickly waved over the waiter, who was standing nearby.

All the young people, sitting on the big stone steps called the Logia, fascinated me. They looked kind of dirty and had loads of tattoos and body piercing and outlandish hair colors. Their behavior was normal, but they appeared odd. GG saw me looking at them and looked alarmed. "Darling, if you only have one chance to make a first impression, what is your first impression of those kids on the steps?"

That seemed like an easy question as I was looking right at a girl with purple hair. "Colorful is how they look to me."

"Yes, that is a good word." She seemed satisfied with my answer, but continued. "What do you want other people's first impression of you to be?"

This question didn't stump me either, but I figured GG had an answer in mind. So I thought for a moment what she might want to hear, then my head popped up and I replied, "Nice, I guess."

"You are nice, and that is exactly what people will think. And some of those kids are probably nice too, but you sure cannot tell that by looking at them." I should have told GG right then that I did not want to look like those kids because she seemed worried, but instead I just smiled and kept on eating.

After finishing our lunch we each had a dish of gelato. Mine was chocolate. Gelato is how they say ice cream in Italy, and it is extra smooth and yummy. As we were finishing up I told GG how much I liked the big art museum that we had visited earlier.

Seeing pretty pictures and these old building was one of the reasons we were visiting Florence, and the Uffizi museum is very famous. "I liked the big Botticelli painting the best." It was huge. It showed a gathering of people standing in the forest and it should have looked weird, but somehow it looked calm and pretty.

"You are not alone with that choice, Abby. People from all over the world come, just like we have, to see these important paintings. That one is called Primavera."

"Like my street in Santa Barbara?"

"The very same." GG was pleased that I had enjoyed the gallery, as she was always telling me about great art and artists. "The most important time for art in Florence was the Renaissance. I have been studying that in my art history class."

GG loves to go to school and is always taking classes to learn something new. She says that is what she enjoys most about her time in London, that they have so many schools and places to learn. I didn't say so, but I think she really likes to live in London because there are a zillion shoe stores.

"The Renaissance was 500 years ago. Artists made beautiful paintings for churches to tell the stories of the Bible. Most of the people did not know how to read so they needed pictures to look at, like comic books on the wall."

"They don't look funny to me," I said.

"No, not like funny comics, I just mean like picture books. The artists also painted beautiful images and portraits to decorate the huge villas of the wealthy Florentines."

"Like the Villa Flurio? I wonder what happened to that man?"

"Yes, Hercules should have let us know by now." GG took a final bite of pizza. "We still have a lot to see today, so if you are finished we better get going." I nodded in agreement.

We left the café and walked fast across the lively piazza. I looked back at our table and noticed GG had left her hat behind. Maybe she realized her new haircut was not so horrible as she had feared. I thought her hair looked pretty, so I quickly turned away and didn't mention the hat. I took her hand as we moved through the jostling crowd.

GG has been to Florence many times and seemed to know all the streets. We walked down a bumpy street made of rocks, and GG said we were going toward the Cathedral. The sun vanished as we turned and made our way down a crowded narrow side street lined with tall shops and apartments.

The buildings along this street seemed to lean inward on each side. "Yikes, GG, these buildings look like they are going to fall over."

"You are perfectly safe; these building have looked like that for 500 years."

There were window boxes way up high with red flowers, and shirts and pants hanging on lines. People were leaning out of high windows, talking across the way. It was so shady I wondered how the clothes were going to dry.

We walked on and a kitten appeared. GG shook her head. "No more kitten adventures, please." We kept walking, but I looked back to see the kitty dart into a shop.

Suddenly, like flipping a light switch, the sun flashed on. After a second for our eyes to adjust, our view was filled with a gigantic white building. Wow, the sheer size of this massive building brought us to a halt. I have never seen such a large place. And just then we both jumped into each other's arms as the bells in the tower started ringing. Large and noisy, this really was a special place.

We made our way to the front façade of the building. It was not easy to enter. We climbed the steep marble stairs to the front doors, but they were covered with weary tourists taking a rest, so it was more like an obstacle course to go inside.

It felt like a gigantic marble cave, and the people inside looked like tiny ants running everywhere. There were not many windows, and they were up high and were covered with colored glass pictures. As it was rather dark, our eyes again had to make adjustments.

GG stopped walking and closed her eyes. I did too. We had gone from bright sunshine to a dark interior. I knew if I closed my eyes they would adjust to the change more quickly. GG kept hers closed a little longer, and a distant peaceful look came on her face.

I moved off to look at more paintings. There were so many people, when GG opened her eyes she thought I was gone. I was nearby. I know not to wander off, as my parents have been telling me that since I first learned to walk. But she looked panicked until I waved at her.

GG joined me under one of the big paintings and asked me if I liked it. It was very large and looked pretty. I said, "Yes. I think that is baby Jesus and his Mom. They look happy."

"You nailed it."

"Look, GG, over there we can light candles for Grandpa Ted," I said, pointing to a little room that seemed to be glowing with hundreds of candles. Once GG told me she was certain that he knew we were thinking about him when we lit candles. Actually, I am pretty certain GG is thinking about him most of the time. He always seems close by and always makes her happy.

"Now time, I think, for us to head back to the hotel to freshen up."

I nodded in agreement. "Freshen up, that means go to the bathroom, right?" Always listening for what adults didn't say as much as what they do say.

"Oh no, in Italy you will find most of the public restrooms are usually very old, but quite acceptable, which is another reason I enjoy visiting here. We do not have to return to our hotel for that."

"Good because I kinda need to go right now."

"Two big Pepsis will do that, kiddo. No problem, there is a lovely little café right across the square. I could use a coffee."

GG pointed out the toilet door, and just as she got comfortable and ordered her coffee I shot right back out of the bathroom. "GG, there is a man in there washing his hands. Either he is lost or I am."

"Don't be alarmed to see a man in there."

"What? We have to use the boy's bathroom here?" I was alarmed. I am not going to do that, I thought.

"No sweetie, don't worry; most of the facilities are for both girls and boys and only the cubicles are private. It will be ok."

I was wide eyed now. "I don't think I like that."

"I agree with you and it takes a bit to get used to, but that is the way it is done in other cultures, especially ones with limited space. Oh and speaking of washing hands, I forgot to mention you must remember the faucet that has the C is the hot water, not the cold. Here the C is for caldo; that means hot in Italian. It is a very unpleasant mistake to make if you get it wrong.

"All done, now let's find a taxi, I am feeling a little tired and think I need to change shoes."

I didn't say anything; I didn't need to, as GG had been limping along for the last half hour. She's a slow learner.

The next several days went by without a single cat sighting or visit to or from the police. Over breakfast GG suggested to me we get out of the city. "I am ready for some wide open spaces, Abby, how about you?"

"Sure, I am ready to be away from all of these cars zipping by. I keep jumping on and off these narrow sidewalks, and I am afraid I am going to land in you know what." I looked at my grandmother, who was shaking her head and making it clear she did not want to reopen the poo conversation.

"Ok, let's get dressed. Then we are off to the countryside." No more than half an hour later we were headed to a taxi stand.

"I hope we don't have to wait too long this time," I said matter of factly as I scanned the streets for an oncoming taxi. In Florence you cannot just wave to a taxi passing by like you can in London or New York. Here you must go to specifically designated taxi stands, and we often had to wait for a taxi to arrive.

A small, white, and freshly washed taxi chugged up and greeted us happily. The driver was delighted when he heard how far we wanted to go.

He drove us zig-zagging through the city, then high into the Tuscan hills above Florence and to the ancient picturesque town of Fiesole. He had good English and gave us a running commentary of the areas we passed on our journey. The driver told us he was not Italian; he was from Iraq.

"That must have been a shocking transition to go from the desert to the Italian countryside?" said GG.

"No, we did not have time for shock," he told us with a shrug. "When it became urgent for us to relocate and our family fled the Middle East, only a few countries had not already filled their quotas but Italy has welcomed us.

After about a half hour we stopped. "You will be able to find a return taxi right here," he said as GG gave him a big tip. We exited the taxi into a large, colorful square. GG brought out a guidebook she had tucked in her tote bag.

We followed her map through the town. It was a small town built into the side of the hills and the streets were twisty. "Here we are, Abby." She pointed to a sign that said "Etruscan ruins and amphitheater."

"This stuff looks really old."

"Make that times a thousand." GG was ruffling the pages of her guidebook as we kept plodding along a dusty footpath. When we stopped at a clearing near the top of the rocky hill, a young uniformed man approached us and asked if we needed a guide. This sounded like an excellent idea, and GG asked how much he charged for his services.

"Forty euros for one hour of tuition," he replied in fairly good English. GG readily agreed and handed over the funds. Then the young man pulled out an identification badge in Italian and told GG that she was in "violation."

"Violation?" GG shrugged and so did I. He turned and pointed to some posted signs in Italian and English that said "Beware, Unregistered Guides Working In This Area. You must secure an authorized ticket before you hire. Fine one hundred euros."

GG quickly mounted a defense claiming entrapment and demanded to see a supervisor.

"I regret that will not be possible today," said the young cop. "You must pay the fine or go to the police station in the square below."

Never one to take unnecessary exercise, GG agreed to his demands. "Ok, I'll pay," she said with disgust as she handed the man another sixty euros and waited for a receipt.

"Lady, you misunderstand; you must pay forty more euros. The fine is one hundred euros."

"I am well acquainted with misunderstandings, young man, and I assure you this is not one." GG was livid.

I glanced sideways at GG. Eyes wide. I could see her hair was a veritable forest fire now as her face had gone almost purple, eyes bulging. I thought GG might actually hit the man, but I hoped not. You would probably get in a lot of trouble for hitting a policeman.

"This is outrageous." GG made no attempt to disguise her fury. "I will pay you so you don't waste another minute of our valuable time, but I shall report you." GG thrust two additional E20. notes at the man, then grabbed her camera and took his photo. "I am a personal friend of Marshal Ridormi, and he shall hear about this."

The young man remained calm and reached out to give GG a pamphlet. Oh no, he's toast, I thought.

Instead, with an expression of revulsion, GG pushed past his outstretched arm and stomped off with me scrambling to follow. Or she tried to stomp, but the stones from the ruins imbedded in the hill made it impossible, even if wearing sensible shoes.

"Abby, when we get back down to the plaza by the taxi stand, remind me I want to make a protest about this. I have his photo so he is going to be in big trouble." In one less confident, these setbacks would whittle away confidence, but not GG armed with her guidebook. We continued our tour as next we visited a 15th Century Franciscan monastery, the Saint Domenico Convent. After walking about in the peaceful courtyard, we visited their gift shop. I bought postcards and a tiny bowl carved from the local marble. Then we stopped by a large fountain and threw in some coins.

GG told me that in the Italian tradition this would ensure we would someday return. "Does that mean return to Italy or to this very fountain?"

"Oh, I think it means back to Italy; we have many more cities and fountains to see".

"Are they on our Grand Tour?"

"Yes, indeed. Now it's time for some lunch. We can't tour without fuel."

"Si, fame de lupo," I said in my best Italian.

"Oh, I have a big surprise now. To complete our visit, we shall have a lavish lunch at the magnificent Villa San Michelle." GG puckered her lips and kissed the tips of her fingers with a big smack. Sometimes when GG says things like lavish it means the menu is full of stuff I don't want. So I was not sure how enthusiastic I was about this surprise, but I was hungry. The San Michele hotel was an old castle on the edge of a cliff. It was kind of neat to be sitting on the terrace, which hung out over the vast valley below. It was very quiet, and I could see no other children.

"Abby, it looks like there is smog in that valley below us," GG sounded alarmed. "How can that be? There is no industry, just miles of vineyards?"

"Maybe from the cars?"

"Possibly, but we are not near any big cities. Just farms with grapes and olive trees roasting in the Tuscan sun."

"Do you know what they raise in the countries where the rainfall is heavy? I asked with a straight face.

"Moss?" she replied tickled with her answer.

"Umbrellas."

"That's a groaner. Did you pull that one on me before?"

"No, that one is from a new book I got at Chaucer's just before this trip."

"You always blindside me with your riddles. Your Grandfather would do that too. You two could have had a TV show with that act." That made her laugh.

Sitting there dangling my legs from the tall, stiff chair, I was kind of day dreaming now as GG began telling me of the many times she and my Grandfather had stayed at this hotel. I knew that nothing made GG so happy as talking about Grandpa Ted. Sometimes it also seemed to make her unhappy. I often wish my grandfather were still alive.

I want GG to always be happy, and also I would like to meet him. It seemed unfair that I never would. My Dad often talks about him and what a really great man he was and that my Dad misses him too. Yes, I think everyone would be happier if Grandpa Ted was still around. Why do people have to die, I wondered, but I didn't ask that day.

GG ordered foie gras parfait starters. When we travel, GG is always ordering things I have never heard of. She doesn't make me eat anything I don't like and is always satisfied if I just take a quick taste. The foie gras looked pretty in a tall, clear glass cup. I didn't ask her what it was and it tasted ok, but I ate very little. Our next course, as

GG would call it, was truffle crusted scallops and asparagus. GG knows I don't like green vegetables so she asked the waiter to remove my asparagus spears, which he put it on a small plate and GG ate them. She told me that scallops are shellfish and truffles were very expensive mushrooms.

To me the truffles smelled kind of like dirty sneakers, but knowing how GG felt about smelly stuff I didn't mention it.

"They send trained pigs out into the woods to find them."

I squinted at her and with a tilt of my head, "Really? Hard to imagine how a pig could learn to collect truffles no matter how well they train them."

"I am absolutely certain. This has been going on for hundreds of years."

"Must be why they are so expensive. All the pig training needed." When I asked how they carried them she just shook her head, signaling the end of the pork and fungus conversation. She did seem to know what she was talking about, but GG always talks with authority even when she really doesn't know what she is talking about at all. My Dad told me that.

The table had many beautiful dishes, and we drank sparkling water with lemon wedges from tall, stemmed glasses. "The aromas, textures, and flavors of this entire meal are intoxicating," GG said with a smile and her eyes closed.

"Sure, GG, if you say so." To me there was a serious absence of mac-n-cheese."

About that time a man walked in that looked a whole lot like Fabio. I turned my head toward GG and raised my eyebrows and jerked my head toward the man. GG squinted and shook her head no. "GG, I wonder what happened to that man and the painting?"

"Me too. The marshal should have updated us by now."

"Does it count as being arrested if the policeman was a fake guide?" I looked at GG with a flat, curious stare.

"Certainly not. Why do you ask such an odd question?"

"My Mom bet my Dad that we would not go one week without getting arrested or visiting the inside of a police station. We already went once."

"We were helping."

"Ok, then does that guide or policeman today count? If not, then my Mom was wrong and my Dad won."

"Won. The whole bet is appalling. Anyway, I don't approve of betting."

"You don't?" I quizzed. "My Dad says you gamble like mad."

"Don't be silly, playing the lottery is a way to help the state pay for schools. It is our duty." Now she was really squirming. "Getting arrested is a horrible thing to make a game of, and I am glad your mother lost. I certainly hope you told them."

I interrupted her, "Yep, misunderstandings, of course I told them." And I turned to my plate as the waiter set dessert before me.

After we had a totally delicious pear tart with cream I was really full. "GG, I think my tummy will explode if I have even one more bite."

"Oh, darling, don't say something so coarse after such an elegant meal, but yes, I am pretty up to the top too. I could really enjoy a nap about now." That was our signal to return to the square to get a taxi back to Florence.

The pretty square was large and also set on the edge of the mountain as our terrace at lunch had. There were red terra cotta planters filled with flowers in every possible color and stone benches and tables with people sitting drinking sodas and playing cards. Children were kicking balls and dogs chasing them. It looked like a fun place where the town peopled liked to hang out.

"GG, we are in luck. Look at that line of ready and empty taxis."

"Great, my nap is getting closer, but first I want to report that phony guide. Do you see a police station?"

"Maybe it is that small place over there." I pointed near the edge of the square.

"Yes, that must be it." We headed that way. When we arrived we could see that the dilapidated abandoned police facility had been boarded up for some time. An official-looking notice posted on the wall referred us to another police service location in case of emergency. There was also a large, once colorful, now peeling, and faded warning flyer posted that read, "Beware of Pickpockets, Beware of False Guides, and Beware of False Policemen."

GG and I were silent for a moment, then we both started to laugh. GG quickly checked her pockets, flapping her hands on her pants. "My money is still safe. It looks like we only got taken for two out of three."

"Is it taxi time?" I asked as GG nodded in reply.

There were lots of taxis, but no luck. We were informed the taxi drivers were on strike.

GG and I looked at each other. That is certainly not what the driver told us earlier. GG turned and looked blankly at the driver of the first car in line. He seemed to be the spokesman for the others, who were intently watching the exchange.

He was a tubby little man with a smiling face, oily from the afternoon heat. His squat frame was shoved behind the wheel of a small taxi many sizes too small for his girth. I wasn't sure how he got in that little taxi or how he would ever get out.

GG was far too relaxed from our meal to want to enter into combative negotiations for transport home, but knew she must. As I mentioned before, if there is a problem she does what it takes to fix it.

I just stood back. GG closed her eyes and took a deep breath. Then opened her eyes slowly and with obvious suspicion of the driver said, "Is this a joke? This is not at all amusing." Believe me, she did not look amused. Then she continued, "A taxi brought us up here not five hours ago."

"Was that perhaps a taxi from Florence?"

"It was. Yes, it was from Florence," I said nodding and hoping to be helpful.

"The drivers from Florence, they are not on strike, only the ones from Fiesole. The drivers in Florence make a great deal more money than we do."

"Ah, I get it," said GG. "How much?" This seemed like a good solution to me, but the driver shook his head.

"Please no, signora, I could not violate the strike. This would be unfair to the other drivers. We are in solidarity."

I was not sure what solidarity meant, but I figured GG did and didn't care.

"One hundred euros," GG bluntly offered him, which I knew was double what we had paid for our trip earlier.

I was sure he would like that so I repeated "One hundred euros." And joined GG in another nod and smile.

"You cannot insult me with your money," said the now indignant driver. Insult? Gosh this is getting intense, I thought.

GG is not the type to back down. "This strike is about money, and I am offering you money. How can that possibly be insulting?" reasoned GG with escalating frustration. Right now I just bet she was feeling the heat from her scalp beginning to singe. I stepped back behind her, not sure what she was going to do next.

GG leaned down and whispered to me, "Go check with that bus driver over there." She pointed to a long bus on the far side of the square. "Find out when the next bus leaves for Florence."

I turned and took off toward the bus. As I crossed the square a soccer ball came right at me, so I return-kicked it and suddenly found myself in the game.

All around were shouts and laughter and I wasn't exactly sure, but it looked like my team was winning. I ran to the other side and helped guard the runner as his foot shot out, and he kicked one right past the goalie. Now we were all cheering. One girl ran over and patted me on the back. The ball was in play again, and I ran toward it while first hopping over a small dog that had joined us.

Just then I looked up and the bus was chugging out of the square. "Oh no, I caused us to miss the bus to Florence."

"No that bus goes to Pisa. The next bus to Florence is in one hour," said one of my teammates. He spoke good English, which he said he studied in school.

I gave the ball one last kick then ran back to GG to explain what I had learned. She was still arguing with the driver.

"Impossible, signora, I cannot," said the driver with a shake of his head. Then his eyes softened, and he smiled at me. "Perhaps one of the young people in the square might be persuaded to drive you to the city."

Tired of this game, GG really thought she was being set up. With no interest in further discussion she gave a seriously cross frown to the driver and asked, "Ok, any suggestions which one might be a safe driver?"

The square was full of the zippy Vespas and for a moment I thought we might get to ride one down the hill.

"No Vespas," GG quickly added. Phooey, I thought.

"I believe the boy with the blue shirt is an excellent driver."

"Fine," GG spat, then turned her back to the driver and gently hugged me near. "In a nutshell, we are stuck."

"What do we do next? Buy the car and drive ourselves?" I asked her cautiously.

That made her roar with laughter. "Now you are thinking like Grandpa Ted, but let's hope it doesn't come to that." I was still waiting to hear her plan.

"I don't like the idea of hitchhiking down the hill, and I think your Dad would kill me if he knew we got in a strange vehicle, but we are out of options."

"We could wait for the bus." Without reply she took my hand and we started across the square.

"Honey, I think when you get back to Santa Barbara you better not mention this misunderstanding to your Dad." GG desperately did not want my parents to learn about things that got messed up.

"GG, you know I am not allowed to tell a lie. What if he asks me?"

GG stopped walking and snapped, "Ask you." She was pretty short tempered about now. "Why would he do that? Never mind." She started walking again, still tightly holding my hand. She stopped again.

"Ok, if your Dad does happen to ask you if we went hitchhiking in the Tuscan hills, by all means go right ahead and tell him, but please don't bring it up first."

"Sure, on the DL it is." She was pretty sarcastic, but I was feeling sorry for her. The cozy calm of our special lunch was now long forgotten and I too just wanted to get back to the hotel.

We made our way back to the other side of the cobblestone square. I waved goodbye to the soccer players as we approached the blue-shirted young man. He was leaning on a tiny and clean, but road weary three-wheel Moped truck. He was talking on his cell phone.

I thought his vehicle was cute and the smallest truck I had ever seen. It looked like the one in the park at home that Penny plays on. Goodie, this is going to be fun. I pulled out the camera to take a picture of it and GG stiffened, "No evidence allowed."

"Sure, the DL." I put the camera away.

The boy quickly closed his phone. He tried to open the door, but had to jerk on the door handle several times before it opened. I tried unsuccessfully not to giggle.

Then with an elaborate bow and with his other arm in a wide gesture of welcome, he invited us to get in the ancient green Ape flatbed. GG took a big gulp of air, put her hand to her forehead and sighed deeply. Then we hopped in.

GG looked at me and winked. Then turning to look at the driver, she asked, "Oh, by the way, how much is this little ride going to cost us?"

With a broad grin he answered, "My father told me you would pay 100 euros." His father?

The next few days were filled with what GG called tourist pursuits. Visits to the Pitti Palace, where the powerful Medici family lived during the Renaissance. Then we went on to two additional huge churches with amazing paintings and candles to light for Grandpa Ted. While not as big as the Duomo, they were still much larger than any church I had ever seen in California. As a special surprise we also visited the Ferragamo Shoe Museum.

I am not making this up. I had no idea there was such a thing as a shoe museum, but was not surprised to find GG knew where one was located. On the way out of the museum we stopped at the bathroom. The stalls were very narrow, so we set our bags on a large marble top table. Others had as well.

When we had finished we grabbed our things and after a brief stop at the gift shop, where we bought charms with shoes on them to hang on my backpack, we headed to the exit. As we were about to step through the doors a security officer grabbed GG.

"Alto, signora."

"Are you mental? And don't you dare touch that child."

GG had swung around and now eyes flaring at the guard she jerked her arm free.

A well-dressed man and woman approach and asked, "Signora, please step into the office." The man was not saying this as a request. You could see in his eyes he was serious.

"What is going on?" GG was baffled. I was unsure if she was mad or what? I stayed close by.

"Signora, we have called the police in this matter and ask you to please wait quietly."

"What matter? This oaf grabbed me and, yes, I want you to call the police. Call Marshal Ridormi."

"As you wish, signora." He nodded to the woman. "This is a serious offense." Then he left the room.

"GG, what's happening?"

"Clearly it is some mis-"

"Understanding?" I said.

"Well yes, exactly." I started looking around the room. On the wall were framed photographs of shoes. And there was a vase in the shape of a boot with red roses inside. The man and woman had been away about 10 minutes, but re-entered the room and stood by the door.

"I demand to know what this is about. I have the marshal's card right here, and I demand you call him at once." She was very cross, then opened her purse and started rummaging about looking for the card. Then she went into slow motion and her head rose up.

"Oh my. There seems to be some mistake. I, I," GG looked at me. Her eyes went limp. "Abby, this isn't my purse." I did a double take and replied with a look of astonishment.

Just then Hercules walked through the glass doors. "Si,

a misunderstanding. That is why Signor Ferragamo has called me."

"I don't know how this happened, but I didn't mean.."

"GG, maybe when we were in the bathroom. There was lots of stuff on the table."

"Not to worry, I have explained to the museum staff that you are a friend of the Questura and that this could not have been intentional."

"You are not going to arrest us are you?" I asked in a panic.

"Arrest Nancy Drew? No. Now please give the purse to them so they can return it to the rightful owner."

GG was still shaken. She lifted the bag from her lap and held it out to the marshal. The woman standing nearby still was not smiling. She then handed GG her purse, which was identical to the one that had been taken.

On the taxi ride back to the hotel I asked, "This doesn't count as arrested, does it?" GG didn't say it, but her eyes said shut up.

On the last full day of our stay in Florence, for breakfast we went to the buffet in our hotel cafe. It was small but filled with eggs, cold meats, cheese, fruit, and two baskets of mini pastry. I loaded my plate, then followed GG to a small corner table. "GG, I wonder whatever happened to that man Fabio?" I was organizing my plate, then took a nibble of fruit. "We should have asked Hercules when we saw him yesterday?"

This made GG laugh out loud. "I don't think that would have been good timing, but I too am curious. Oh, and better not mention that part of the trip to your parents. GG took a fork full of scrambled eggs.

I mouthed, "The DL." I was certain my Mom had won the bet.

We finished our meal and discussed our plans for the day, and we both agreed we had seen quite enough art and artifacts. GG suggested we resort to what she said is the most touristy of all activities, going shopping.

GG always finds time to shop and since we were running out of time, today had to be the day. Our first stop was the San Lorenzo Street Market. This is an outdoor jumble of trader stalls that circles the Church of San Lorenzo. It has a bewildering number of options.

"This place holds another of Florence's great secrets," teased GG as she nodded to the stalls. "This shamble of cheap goods masks the astounding beauty created by Michelangelo, which is just below our feet in the Medici tombs." She stomped her foot. We don't have time to see them on this visit, but we certainly will on our next."

"We are coming; back the fountain said so," I said with a laugh. She did too and gave me a hug.

I liked the energy of the crowded market. There were lots of children playing and dogs barking and darting in and out of the displays and pushy barkers touting the goods.

I was surprised GG had brought me here. She never enjoyed these types of places, but she said it was famous. Usually I do not like to shop. My Mom does and she has just dragged me to one too many boring stores. But this was not boring, which I guess was because it was outside and rather chaotic.

I chose several small packages of the famous Florentine writing paper for my Mother. She sends lots of emails, but she also writes lots of notes on paper, which I have heard is special and kind of rare these days.

I found a Leonardo Da Vinci Vitruvian Man t-shirt for my Dad. The drawing reminded me of the plans and blueprints he is always looking at. For my best friends Lauren and Kora I bought tote bags with a picture of the Duomo and for my little sister, a hat that said "I heart Firenze."

"Oh GG, this will look so cute on Penny." I held the hat up for inspection.

"It certainly will, but truthfully even a paper hat would look delightful on such a cute cherub." I was missing Penny.

"Ok, we are done here. We don't want to spend any more of our time prowling through this tat." And we headed to the luxurious designer shops on Via Tornabuoni.

GG was stunned as we walked along the fashionable boulevard. Looking inside, all the windows were all dressed with the color GG had called ghastly, which I had tried to wear to dinner at Buco Maria a few evenings earlier. I looked at GG, who had her nose wrinkled up. "I told you so," I said with a big smile.

"Ok, Miss Fashion Smartie, you win. But you have to agree, it is not one of God's rainbow." Then as we moved to the next shop she stopped and said, "Oh my, the color is positively everywhere. And look, all the garments are missing a sleeve!" GG knew when she was beaten. "Let's go in," she sighed, "I think I need a makeover."

"Like you did with your hair," I added. And with a big grin GG just shook her head in defeat and held the door as we walked into the cool interior.

Later, exhausted, we headed to the nearby city center, the Piazza Republica for much-needed refreshments. We were laden with dozens of designer shopping bags and totes. GG said we looked like cosmopolitan Sherpa.

"What's a Sherpa?"

"More like who. They are the local people who carry all of the gear up Mount Everest for the climbers." She also said with a laugh that she was certain they had far less to carry than we had.

"I might need to buy an extra suitcase to get all of this home," she said as she nodded at our parcels. "I am still hoping for us to find my missing bag. Though there is not any spare room in it. First, help me pick a place for us to sit down and get a snack."

I thought the one near the big merry-go-round in the square looked fun, but I didn't mention it. I know GG pretty well, and she would not like it. GG preferred demure places, she had told me, ones with just a few well-behaved children, not kids hollering from a noisy carousel. "Let's see, which place shall we choose?" said GG as her glance swept the square. "Gilli's, of course, it is the best place on the square, perhaps even the best in the city, and we are both dressed up." So off we went across the crowded square, which was an obstacle course of bicycles, clots of tourists, dog poo, and enormous potholes.

At Gilli's, things were elegant and calm. There was a window full of yummy cakes and candies; this looked like a perfect choice to me. We were warmly greeted and quickly seated at one of the small draped tables on the terrace. The late afternoon sun was still warming the piazza, and the music from the street was echoing throughout the square. It was almost like a party going on all around us. GG was right. I like Florence.

GG was feeling very content I could tell because she was smiling sweetly right at me. She told me she had waited years to show Florence to me. "Abby, with the exception of the odd events at Villa Flurio it has been a perfect week."

"And the stolen purse, the fake guide, and the taxi strike."

"None of that was our fault and doesn't count at all. Really, just forget about that."

"Sure, GG. It was a pretty weird night at the Villa. I wonder whatever happened, and why the marshal never told us."

"Oh, I am sure it is all happening behind the scenes. They are not really allowed to tell. But we did our part, and I am proud of that."

"And he did come and rescue us at the shoe museum."

"Abby, I am really happy to be sitting here with you. And what do we always do on the last day of our little trips?"

Thinking that was an easy question I quickly answered, "Decide what story I am allowed to tell Dad about what we did?"

"Ha-ha, you do have quite a vivid imagination."

"Yes, I know I do; my Dad tells me I take after you," I said with genuine pride.

Ignoring me and hoping to return to more positive conversation, she said, "What we always do on our last day is plan where we are going next. Do you have any suggestions? I know I have a few."

"Oh, you know you never take my suggestions."

"What can you mean; don't I always ask you?"

"Yes, you always ask alright, GG, but we always go to where you want to go."

"I suppose it could seem that way, it is just that I have seen so many amazing places and want to share them with you."

"True, you do know some neat places."

"And if I remember, last time I asked, you suggested for our next trip we should go to Velveeta, Kansas, where your friend Elise's grandmother lives. Isn't this nicer?"

"She lives in Colby, and Kora and Elsie say it is a fun place. They have cows."

"Cows, exactly my point." GG sounded sarcastic.

"I have had a good time here, so I guess I will let you choose the next place too." I knew that planning our next trip was really important to GG, and she did have good ideas.

"Ok, that's settled. Darling, I have had a marvelous time too. In fact, this calls for an ice cream sundae." She then turned to signal a waiter and take in the view of the lively square.

I was looking around too. There were pigeons in the square trying to sneak into our area. Seated next to our table on the terrace was a man in a business suit reading the International Tribune English-language newspaper. I read the headline. "Contessa Lamberti Dies After Lengthy Illness," and there was a photo of an elderly man and woman.

"GG, what was the name of the man in the Villa Flurio?"

"Count Lamberti. Why do you ask?"

"That's what I thought, but look." I pointed to the paper. GG turned and was startled to see the large photo on the front page. "What!" She lunged and grabbed the paper from the astonished gentleman's hands and shouted, "This is not Count Lamberti! Count Lamberti is young and handsome!"

The businessman was trying to retrieve his paper, but GG held on. Then she jumped up, which caused the paper to rip in two. Trying to get out of the way of GG's assault, he bumped the table and sent his coffee and Panini sandwich flying.

"Oh no, we must tell the marshal. Conto rapido!" shouted GG in near hysterics while waving wildly at the waiter, who stood by totally confused as we had not yet ordered and she was yelling for the bill.

"Abby, please quickly, give me your phone," GG demanded while waving her arms.

"No phone. You told me I had to leave it in our room; it is one of your rules." I turned my palms up and down to show there was no phone hidden there. Yikes, she is losing it, I thought.

"Yes, yes, it is a rule, but now we must go quickly to the police station." GG scanned the square, and as usual the taxi stand had a long queue of people waiting and not one taxi in sight.

I was feeling a bit worried now, as GG seemed to be ranting wildly, saying all kinds of things that made no sense at all. She took off and was also practically running in the high heels she insisted on wearing on our last day. She was wobbling so much I was sure she was going to topple over.

"Stop, GG, we are forgetting our packages," I shouted. "Wait for me." I had never seen my grandmother move so fast.

GG circled back to our table. The businessman saw her charging again and moved far clear. GG scooped up an armload of bags. She turned to the businessman and said, "Sorry, gotta run," and she laid some euros on his table, then took off again.

"Grab the other packages, we have to go now," she shouted over her shoulder as she fled. I turned to the man holding half a newspaper and mouthed "sorry," then ran to catch up.

On the nearby Piazza Strozzi GG shouted, "A miracle has occurred!" She pointed to a lone taxi waiting with no one in line. GG knocked on the grimy window, then grabbed my hand and with our bundles we jumped inside. Time was short, and it was clear after her run through the streets her feet were in agony.

"To the Carabinieri station at Piazza Ognissanti pronto, per favore!" she shouted. To which the lifeless driver just shrugged and pulled away from the curb at a plodding pace.

Florence is a maze of narrow one-way streets and too many cars, so the trip to the station seemed to take forever. When we finally arrived, we bolted from the taxi and went running into the station with bags and voices flying. Not remembering to pay the driver, he showed previously unrevealed urgency by rapidly following us into the station. Waving his arms and angrily shouting at us and the officers.

One of the young Carabinieri stepped forward and asked GG for eleven euros and tried to calm the situation. She responded with a sharp look, then grabbed a handful of notes from her bag, not bothering to count them and shoved them at the driver. "Here, now go away." Excitedly, GG addressed the two regally dressed officers at the desk, "Please, I must speak to Marshal Ridormi. It is an emergency."

"I am sorry signora, but the marshal is having his lunch and cannot be disturbed until after 4:30. You may wait in the chairs by the window," the duty officer calmly explained.

"What! Not even for an emergency?" I asked.

"No, signorina, not even for an emergency, should one actually exist," smoothly answered the man. GG shook her head and threw her hands in the air, but said nothing.

I was sitting in a chair, swinging my legs, and wondering what was going to happen next. GG was anxiously pacing the small area in front of the desk. She walked to the window and deep in thought looked out at the busy courtyard of the station. The officers were staring at her now with awed curiosity about this eccentric American with the vivid imagination.

I knew GG had been ignored far too long. She turned on her heels and said loudly, "This is madness. Murder and theft cannot wait for lunch. I demand at once you tell him that Miss Marple is here."

With this, the head of one young officer snapped up and he said, "Did you say Miss Marple? Of course, I will summon him at once. You are very famous here at our humble station. Momento, per favore," he said as he exited the room. GG always knows how to get people to pay attention to her.

When the tall marshal entered the room, GG had barely begun to calm from her breathless and enthusiastic entrance to the Questura. I was still unsure what was going to happen.

Marshal Ridormi was by contrast quite relaxed and slowly putting on his immaculate jacket, which he must have removed to eat his meal.

"Yes Miss Mar, signora, please, what is so urgent I am not able to finish my coffee? Surely you have not been arrested again?"

GG ignored his question and asked, "What day is today?

"Thursday, but I am sure you did not need me for that," he replied exasperated by the question.

"That is Giovedi, right? My Italian is a bit rusty, and I lose track of days when on holiday. I must know if this is Giovedi?"

"Si, it is Thursday, Giovedi," he assured her. "Why are you so distressed, signora?"

"Marshal, the crime at the villa. You have been investigating haven't you?"

"Yes, signora, and your information has been most helpful."

"Well, your case is about to break wide open! The man we thought I saw in the Villa Florio was not the Count. At 8:00 tonight you will have your killer and art thief. "

Then Hercules waited for GG to continue. "At Gilli's on the Piazza Republica, the man I saw in the villa has a date tonight with a beautiful woman."

The marshal and I were both quite mystified now. He raised his eyebrows in confusion. He looked at me and then back at GG. "Who?" we said in unison.

"We just have a few hours to set it all up." GG was smiling broadly, her head was suddenly popping with ideas, and she was determined to be a big part of this. "Let's go get him!" Her face was flushed with excitement as she told of her ideas, waving her hands in a very Italian way. Everyone in the reception area was now watching her with great interest. She was amazing.

"This is a most colorful story and very much as we have come to expect from you, Signora Gable, but now you must tell it to me again, more slowly. Please to my office?"

"Carlo, bring us two coffee," said the marshal as he leaned back in his chair.

"And for Abby a Pepsi, per favore," said GG. Excellent idea; I was very thirsty from all that was going on.

At this request Ridormi smiled and nodded to Paolo and then turned to GG to hear her plan. I too wanted to know what was going on in her head.

While we sipped our drinks, GG explained how and what we knew about the activities of the dashing villain, the handsome man from the plane. They even asked me to look at some photos and if any of them looked like the mean man from the street below our window or from inside the villa the night we were watching from the dark gardens.

I told the marshal they all looked mean to me and I couldn't really tell. He assured me it was ok if I wasn't certain or did not recognize any. I kept looking at the pages, then when I flipped to almost the last page there he was.

I almost jumped out of my seat when I saw him. "Aak! That's him for sure," I said while pointing at his photo. The marshal smiled at me, and GG smiled at the marshal.

GG confirmed my choice, "I told you she was one smart cookie." Then the marshal nodded at two of his officers, who quickly left the room.

When GG had finished telling the marshal everything she knew, he made us promise not to go anywhere near Gilli's for the remainder of the day. After securing an agreement from GG to return to our hotel, he sent us on our way.

GG had readily agreed we would not go to the Piazza Republica, but nothing would be sufficient to keep someone as nosey as GG from missing this event and what she told me was called the take down.

"Come on, Abby, we need to get into position, but first I need to wash up and to change my shoes." We were rapidly crossing the piazza in front of the hotel.

"I thought the marshal told us to stay away?" I did not like the idea of breaking a promise, and especially not to a policeman.

"Oh yes, true, but they might need our help, and we don't want to be too far away, do we?" My Dad says GG excels in the art of justification so her explanation sort of made sense, but I was suspicious she might get us into trouble again, and my Dad really gets cross when that happens.

After a refreshing stop at the hotel, where we deposited our shopping bags, we washed up and both changed our clothes and shoes. We soon headed out again.

Exiting the hotel, GG grabbed my arm and u-turned us back inside. She made a beeline for the front desk. Smiling and always happy to do whatever GG asked, Massimo agreed to confirm our morning flight and offered to assist in any way. GG then asked if there was any news on her lost bag, to which Massimo with sad, downcast eyes shook his head no. GG assured him we needed nothing more and as usual she gave him a fistful of money. More smiling.

I don't believe I have ever seen my Grandmother quite so energetic. I liked it, but still was worried that if the marshal found out about her plan he would be angry and arrest us or something. The whole idea seemed reckless. I am a pretty mellow kid, and this is not really my style.

We took a taxi from our hotel and returned to the Piazza Republica. The driver dropped us on a far corner of the plaza. We made our way on foot across the busy square, walking right in front of Gilli's. This made me a bit nervous, as this is exactly where we were not supposed to be. We kept going right up to the large upscale department store that I had not noticed when we were nearby earlier.

Once inside GG and I marched on, navigating the ground floor cosmetics and handbags without slowing. GG never gave them a look. This was unusual behavior for her. I hurried to keep up. We went through the store and directly to the escalators on the back wall and rode up three floors.

Next we crisscrossed and weaved through a large room of colorful dresses and coats. Our pace quickened. We also swiftly brushed by several large displays of beautiful shoes and GG did not slow down. Highly unusual.

Just to be certain my grandmother had seen the shoes, I touched her arm, causing her to look over her shoulder at me. GG looked at the shoes, shook her head, and kept going. No shoes, not today. Her target was close, and GG had only one thing on her mind.

Tucked in the back corner with little notice was a narrow wooden staircase. It did not look like anyone was supposed to use it, but GG seemed to know just where she was going, and charged right up. I followed.

It was a further climb up two flights of stairs to the very top of the building, finally emerging onto a small terrace café high above the square. GG took a big breath of air, turned, and said to me, "We did it. This is one of my favorite places in Florence."

"Wow, this is some view, GG, but I thought you didn't like to be up high. How did you find this place?"

"That is true, I don't usually like to be up high, but this place is an exception. And it is not at all well known, or at least not by tourists." Feeling very clever GG added, "The marshal will never know we are here." GG sighed and plopped down.

"Good call, GG. The entire piazza and Gilli's are right below us and will give us a perfect view."

"Check it out, you can see the Duomo over that way," she said as she pointed off to the right. That dome is huge. I had read at school that really big things like the Great Wall of China can be seen from outer space, and I was fairly certain this dome could be seen from the moon.

The sun was fading now. The terrace was almost deserted. It was like being up high in a fancy tree house. The umbrellas were down, and the crisp white tablecloths reflected the glow of the candles that had been lit on every table. The first evening stars began to twinkle above us, and the colorful lights of the shops and carousel danced on the warm, ancient stone walls. It felt magical to me, and when I told GG she put her hands together in silent applause and nodded in agreement.

"Abby, you see the golden light glowing in the square

below? It is very famous and for centuries inspired great artists. It inspires me to paint too, but sadly you need a scrap of talent to make it come to fruition. And I have zip."

I looked to her in sympathy and repeated, "zip," as I relaxed back in my chair.

"Listen, Abby. The evening street troubadours have begun their serenades. I am not sure Bohemian Rhapsody would have been my choice, but it is nice to have music." GG really did love this place.

"Let's get the waiter to bring us two large gelato tri-colore." I nodded at that superb idea. Then GG wiggled around and got comfy in her chair before kicking off her shoes.

The time was passing at a lazy pace. The gelato was yummy, but now long gone and still nothing had happened in the square. I leaned back in my chair and pulled my sweater tight around me. The wind had picked up, and the ice cream had made me cold. I leaned over to warm my hands on the candle just to tease GG because I could tell they were fake. It made her smile.

It was probably not very long, but waiting is boring. I was swinging my legs, trying to stay awake. I didn't have anything to do but just sit there, when suddenly GG lifted her tote into her lap, dug deep inside, and you guessed it, retrieved a guide book she had apparently been hauling around. I smiled at her. And she smiled back smugly as if to say, see carrying these around is a good idea.

At least it was something to do. I took it and found a section called Kids in Florence. As I was reading, I did find some neat stuff. For one thing, you can rent those Vespas just about everywhere. Gosh, I thought, if I ever come here with my Dad I am sure he will take us for a ride. I turned down the corner of the page.

"Hey, what is the Hope School gang up to? Any more kittens to give away?"

I looked up from the guidebook, then set it on the table. "No, GG, but we did give all the others away. Nathan had a Karate competition and couldn't help, but Brooke and I went to the shopping plaza with a mesh baby bed and put the kittens inside with some yarn and some toy mice. My Dad bought bags of food and kitty litter, and we made a big sign with balloons: 'free kittens, food, and free litter.' Jason was our first customer and he took three, one each for Taylor, Jessie and Angie. It took all afternoon, but we gave them all away, and one lady even wanted the baby bed."

"That was clever marketing."

"I wish we had taken some lemonade to sell; all the people walking by looked thirsty and so were we."

"Always an entrepreneur. Abby you will be our family's first billionaire," that made GG smile real big.

I glanced over at a clock on the piazza wall. "It's 8:00, should we be looking over the wall yet?" I was impatient for the main event.

"No, time means nothing in Italy. Those two will not even consider showing up before 8:30 and probably closer to 9:00."

"Sounds like the perfect place for my Mom; she is always late.

"Being late is terribly rude; at least it is in America. People that do that are just trying to get attention." I went back to my guidebook.

"I know, Abby, how about we just have another ice cream."

The first bowl of gelato had been pretty big and I was already full, but it was something to do. "Make mine chocolate this time, please."

Waiting is boring. I was growing tired of leg swinging and toe tapping, so I began finger thumping and humming. Suddenly I straightened up. "I will now do the telephone number from Bye-Bye Birdie." I popped up and in our small corner started to sing softly and dance. This made GG sit up and laugh. She put the book back in her bag.

"Bravo. Excellent performance." She was cheering. "Encore. Better still, it is time to begin our watch."

GG stood up. I took another bow, then stretched tall and leaned out over the wall. "Whoa, not so far." GG grabbed my legs and pulled me back. "It's a long way down. Keep one foot flat on the ground."

I leaned over again, though this time not so much. Very soon the fireworks began. The police cars raced into the square with sirens screaming and lights twirling just like on TV.

Out from Gilli's marched Fabio, the man from the plane, with hands cuffed behind him. Marshal Ridormi led him to a waiting car. Before he got in the car the marshal looked up high, right at us. We both jumped back with a shriek and started laughing.

We loudly hooted and clapped and cheered. We were jumping up and down. "GG, how did he know?" I asked just as a man emerged from the shadows near the back of the dark terrace wall. We turned and saw Officer Scotti with a broad grin as he wagged his finger at us.

"Officer Scotti, we had plenty to share, you should have joined us for ice cream."

"GG, I think Marshal Ridormi did not trust us to stay out of the square tonight." I turned to the officer. "You are not going to arrest us, are you?" I raised my hands in surrender, but GG quickly pushed them down.

"No, we would not arrest Miss Abigaile, our star witness and a great dancer." I blushed as he had apparently seen my song and dance.

"Thank you, that was very kind of you to quietly stand by. Now, can you give us a ride back to our hotel? My feet are killing me."

There were several pictures of the bad guys in the square in the morning papers. GG had tucked the Il Gazzetino in her luggage to show off back home. We were not mentioned by name, but the article had said some American tourists had assisted with information that had led to the apprehension. That was good enough for us.

The Carabinieri had been very grateful for our help and even offered to deliver us to the airport the next morning.

"You know why they made that offer, don't you, Abby?"

I shook my head.

"Because they want make sure we actually get on the plane." She was laughing.

"I hope I can tell everyone about a ride in an Italian police car?" I wasn't sure if GG wanted anyone to know.

"Of course you can. We are heroes. We will even take a photo."

"This time evidence is ok?"

"Absolutely."

We were checking in for our flight from Florence to Rome. GG suddenly twirled. "Abby, one more quick look for my bag with the special strap."

"GG, you sure are the optimistic type. That bag is in Hong Kong or Greenland by now."

"You are probably right, but I am not going to give up."

GG looked at me and grabbed me in a big embrace. "I adore you, Abby, and spending almost a week together in Florence was even more enjoyable than even I have always imagined it would be."

"Me too. We are a good travel team, and there were only a few misunderstandings."

GG shook her head as if to shake those away.

"GG, this 21st Century Grand tour is a lot of fun."

"Next stop Rome."

Rome, Italy

"Abby, I am sorry we don't have time to see Rome again. Though it was fun to share with you when you came to Europe for the Olympics. It is a magnificent city, one of my favorites, well worth many visits." I was thinking they are all her favorites.

"Do you remember the Coliseum and Saint Peter's Basilica? Oh, and the Treve Fountain."

"Oh sure, that was the fountain Penny wanted to swim in."

"It was pretty hot that day, but luckily your Dad grabbed her just before she cannon balled in." We both laughed at the memory.

"I remember flying those light rockets up in the sky in front of the Spanish steps."

"Have you studied about Rome yet? The famous Roman Emperors and the Caesars?" I nodded yes.

GG was off again. I was half surprised she did not bring out a stack of guidebooks. We had flown a short hop from Florence to Rome, but were not leaving the airport. She did point out the Coliseum as we flew above before landing.

In Rome we would catch a non-stop flight to Miami. That is the closest airport to GG's Fisher Island home and also where my Dad and Penny were meeting us. We were heading off to Disney World, which GG calls a Mouse Trap and says she is happy to avoid being snapped, so she wouldn't be joining us.

First thing, we had to deal with our luggage again. The airline in Florence refused to check our bags all the way through to Miami. So we were required to go through the check-in process again. "Abby, look out for my missing bag." I thought that was pretty much a hopeless idea, but nodded that I would.

When we were not able to find a porter, a young man helped us load our bags on the weight scales, and as usual GG's luggage was overweight and she had to pay extra.

"Grazie," she said as she handled the guy a handful of euros. He seemed a bit surprised, but happy with the money. GG said he looked like a student traveling on a budget and perhaps we had bought him a nice dinner.

"I hope he has enough left after dinner to buy some Tylenol. Those bags weigh a ton. I bet he will have a back ache."

GG ignored me. "That helpful young man was a good reminder that the world is full of nice people and not to worry about a few bad people like the baddies we ran across in Florence."

"GG, when we get to the lounge, can I call my Dad?"

"Of course, we should call him. Is your phone charged up?" I nodded yes.

"We are heroes. I am certain he would want to know that. Let's see, what time is it there? We don't want to wake him up."

I quickly did the math in my head. "Remember, he is in

Florida and not California, and that means we are hours closer to the same time."

"I think we are safe. My Dad and Penny both like to sleep late and are up by now." I was happy that I would be talking to him and seeing them soon.

The airport was quiet as it had been in Florence, but the security lines here did not seem as onerous as at the USA screening. The routine was easier, no pat downs or shoe removal. GG always liked to take the easy way, but she said, "This seems too easy, who knows what unstable types may be allowed aboard?" She laughed.

"What does that mean?" I wondered.

"Oh, nothing scary, sweetie, everyone looks nice. Even John Wayne over there." GG got a big smile on her face and winked at me.

"Who?" I was suspicious now.

"John Wayne was a cowboy famous for keeping all the girls safe." GG likes to flirt, so I figured she thought that guy was handsome. I just fluttered my eyes at her, which made her laugh.

Travel seems to be a lot of waiting in lines, but finally we made it through Passport Control, where I got another stamp.

"GG, let me see all your passport stamps?"

"Clever girl. No you cannot. You are just trying to find my name," or age, thought GG.

"I am going to ask my Dad what your real name is."

"He won't tell you. I swore him to secrecy when he was a little boy, and so far he never has told. I will tell you someday."

"Over there, GG, a sign to our lounge."

In the lounge we helped ourselves to some snacks and beverages, then I pulled out my phone and hit my speed dial.

"Buorno giorno, Pappa, it's me."

"What a nice surprise, Cupcake, sounds like you have gone native."

"We are at the Rome airport. We had so much fun in Florence. We caught an art thief who stole a painting with a bunch of naked flying babies, and the police were everywhere and then we.."

"Great honey, about that, let me talk to GG."

"Ok." I got cut off from my story, and he didn't sound very happy.

"Mother, police again. Really? What is going on? A few hours ago, the dad of one of Abby's friends reported that his daughter had received a rather alarming text from Abby. Sounded a lot like what she just told me."

GG quickly turned her eyes to me for signs of betrayal. "Texting," she mouthed silently.

Texting in the room was not on the list of rules, was it? Maybe my text got scrambled flying over the Atlantic Ocean?

GG shook her head quickly while still talking to my Dad. "But son, there must be some misunderstanding," again GG attempted to explain. By this time, her voice had taken a false high pitch sound that my Dad told me he always knew meant trouble his mother was attempting to conceal.

"Yes of course, a misunderstanding. There always is with you, Mother, but there simply cannot be any more of them."

"Son, we are heroes, really."

"Ok, but please no more. Let me say goodbye to Abby."

"Dad, GG really …"

"I don't blame you at all, Cupcake, I love you a bunch."

"Love you too and give Penny a kiss." As I hung up the phone the loud speaker announced our flight was ready to board. More lines.

Once on board the behemoth aircraft we were seated in pods of three. All GG really cared about, she told me, were that we were seated together and that seats were wide and comfy for the long journey ahead. They looked great to me; I expected to sleep all the way.

"I wish that large wood Duomo and Bell Tower you bought had fit in the luggage," said GG. "I am not exactly sure where we are going to put it. Try under the seat."

"I think it will work if I lay it on the side. And anyway I want to look at it."

"Ok, but it has to be put away for take-off. For now, play with the Air Hostess Barbie you bought for Penny at the airport."

"What sounds good to eat?" GG handed me the First Class Air Menu, which had been left with our amenities kits.

"Anything ordinary. We ate a lot of fancy Italian food this week."

"Forget all about that, sweetie," said GG "I am sure we can get you a nice ham sandwich. GG held the menu and motioned to the flight attendant standing at the galley door.

I thought the lady looked kind of old to be working on a plane, but didn't say so. When the attendant finally reached us GG asked, "Your menu is nice, but my young companion would love a sandwich for lunch. Can you please arrange that?"

"No, sorry. In first class we are serving salmon en croute or Chicken Truffle Cannelloni."

Phooey, more of those pig mushrooms, I thought.

"Isn't there an extra sandwich in the back that might find its way up here?" playfully coaxed GG.

"No, that is not possible; there is a strict number allocated."

"Well, can you at least offer the salmon or Cannelloni and see if someone would like to change with her?" said a perturbed, but still smiling GG.

"Did you pre-order a special meal?" asked the attendant.

"No, I did not. I am simply asking for some consideration for my granddaughter, and you are making it very difficult," snapped GG.

"I will be happy to provide you with a formal complaint card," she answered and turned away.

"Fine!" said GG, "and if you will slap it between two pieces of bread and smear it with a little mayo I am sure it will be as tasty and nutritious as the sandwiches you offer in back!" GG was quite overheated by this time.

My eyes were wide with astonishment. "GG, that's ok, that lady did not seem very nice, and we don't want to make her mad." I was trying to make this problem go away.

"I'm the one that's mad, and these tickets cost a bundle, we are not asking for much."

"Really, GG, it is ok, but I am kind of thirsty." As we were now underway I reached down and brought my Duomo replica from under the seat.

The stewardess had retreated to the galley with

considerably more energy than she had shown arriving. Her arms were swinging with determination as she made it up the aisle.

"I am sorry, Abby, but she made me mad. Tough as old boots that one. I don't think you are getting anything simple. Just eat what you want and I will give you my dessert too."

The plane was cruising smoothly, and beverages were being served all around. So far none had been offered to us.

"That old grouch probably told the others to ignore us," said GG, and she reached over and pushed the call button.

"On my flight over, one helped a lady that got some peanuts stuck in her throat."

"Ok fine, they are full of help, but apparently not today." GG was getting a little crabby because I was defending the cabin attendants. Finally someone, a man, came and asked what we needed, but I was dozing against the seat back.

"We would appreciate some beverage service. I would like a sparkling water with ice and a hot chocolate for her, please." GG jerked her head once toward me. "Oh, and any chance of a ham sandwich?" she added in a pleasant tone she did not feel. Big smile.

"I believe it has already been explained to you that ... "

GG interrupted, "Fine, fine, just the drinks, please, and if you could hurry I have a pill to take." GG did not really have a pill to take, but she hoped this would make him move faster.

Wanting to think about anything else, GG looked about the other passengers in our area. What luck, John Wayne was seated right next to her. Then she noticed he was eating a sandwich.

I was awake now, and she whispered to me, "Where did he get that?" She discreetly pointed at Wayne.

Leaning in his direction with a flirty smile she said, "Excuse me, I see you are having a sandwich; where did you get that highly prized item?"

Before he had a chance to answer, the original unhelpful attendant came toward us. I now stirred around and reached out for my hot cocoa, but the lady said she wanted to set it on the tray, as it was very hot.

GG had unbuckled her seat belt and was trying to straighten her sweater. The attendant eyed GG with a smirk. "Please keep your seatbelt fastened when seated, or if it feels too snug we can get you an extender."

GG raged, her cheeks flushed. "Wait just a minute, my seat belt is not as snug as yours I am certain, and where oh where is my drink?" GG added rather too loudly in her frustration.

I slowly sipped my hot cocoa and watched my grandmother over the rim of the cup. I was concerned about her. I knew she was really getting angry; bet her hair is frying, I thought. I looked at GG's glaring eyes and tightly pursed lips.

John Wayne was attempting to conceal his smile when the stewardess said, "We are authorized to refuse service to any passengers we feel are being disruptive, so please do not raise your voice again."

"Oh, for heaven sake, I just wanted a ham sandwich and beverages, please." GG raised her hands and begin to massage her temples, hoping to rub away some of her tension and frustration.

"GG, you look just like that Scream picture we saw in New York."

"You are so right; I'm sure I do." This little exchange had made her smile and also the fact that her art education of me seemed to be working, all of which caused her to relax a bit.

At this, John Wayne, seated next to GG, leaned forward to stifle a laugh, and when his jacket fell open I glimpsed what I was certain was a gun. GG saw it too.

GG's protective instinct kicked in, and her imagination took off at a gallop. "Gun!" she shouted.

"Gun!" I shouted.

"He has a gun!" said GG as she stomped the pointy heel of her towering shoes into the top of his foot.

John Wayne shouted, then slammed GG forward across his lap, and when GG flopped over she sank her sturdy teeth deep into his fleshy leg. This unleashed a catastrophic chain reaction.

Seeing GG under siege, I flung the remaining very hot cocoa into the man's face. I had unlatched my seatbelt when I bent down to retrieve my Duomo, so I popped up with a mighty lunge at him and fiercely thrust the stiff leg of the Air Hostess Barbie far up his flaring nostril. GG was kicking her legs wildly. I climbed right on her back and grabbed the top of the man's hair as his nose now splattered blood everywhere.

The man wailed in agony, but did not release GG. He looked furious. I kept pulling his hair, but he would still not release her. I leaned over and bit his ear and didn't let go. Just then, a seedy-looking man directly across the aisle from us rose up and headed right over the top of his seat. I then noticed his hands were cuffed behind him with zip-ties. I was not sure what was happening, but it was happening very quickly.

In his awkward flight, the man landed on an enormous

soft pet carrier in the row behind and the squeals and howls of the squashed prized Siamese show cats filled the air.

The cats' owner, a woman in the seat next to the cosseted kitty cage was a prim and portly woman. She had been writing thank you notes to the eminent judges of the prestigious Rome cat show, where the now howling cats had taken top prize.

The protective pussies' owner's instincts raged as she jammed her expensive slim line ballpoint pen deep into the ear of the fleeing man, which halted him abruptly.

In the row behind the kitties, a man bravely stood up and grabbed the greasy ponytail of the man now holding his head and screaming in agony from his pierced eardrum.

John Wayne was trying to unlatch his seatbelt, while pushing me away and holding GG down. We had six arms and six legs in this scrum, but it seemed like a lot more as they were all flying and pushing in every direction.

A well-dressed man who had been originally seated directly next to the cuffed and now fleeing man entered the fracas. He moved to the aisle where GG's head now protruded and I hurled the balsa wood Duomo and Bell Tower model at his head. He batted it away, but not before the steeple had gashed his left eyebrow, which was soon squirting blood. GG raised her fists with fury into him, knocking his elbow into a tray an attendant was trying to remove from the scuffle. A fork flew up from the food tray and hit the man's eye just below his gashed eyebrow. At this assault, the man let out a yelp that silenced even the wailing felines.

The coach class passengers in the far back were unaware of the events up front, busily enjoying their club sandwiches and juice, but the nearer business class passengers had been alerted to the pandemonium. With the shouts and scuffle in progress the Business passengers feared what might be happening, and three burly men and a tiny old woman armed with an umbrella she was flailing stormed the First Class area, knocking over two cabin attendants trying to calm the situation. They all fell into a heap.

The intercom barked with authority, as the pilot made a hasty announcement and demanded everyone remain in his or her seat and stay calm. GG was then cuffed with zip ties and escorted to the forward area behind the pilots' cabin. There, with a sinking heart, GG was strapped into a fold-down seat. Another outburst of indignation, no matter how justified, was just too much work. With the miasma of defeat swirling around her, arms limp and her head slumped forward in shame she was told to stay quiet for the remaining seven hours of the flight. I felt worried about her and worried about what my Dad was going to say if he found out. And he always found out.

GG told me once that my Dad had worked out a good system for having a quiet life, and did not want anyone interfering with it. And did not appreciate her misunderstandings, which he called hare-brained adventures that disrupted his own life. GG hinted my Dad had not near enough adventure in him these days; he took his parenting duties, work, and even his hobbies very seriously and left little room for serendipity. As I looked at GG trussed up like a criminal, I thought he made a lot of sense.

The aircraft landed safely in Miami. The other passengers deplaned in silence, while many gave us harsh looks. GG was told she would have to wait for her escort. The harsh demands of the cabin attendants had failed to shake my resolve to remain at GG's side. The attendant had told me I was in trouble too for my role in the upheaval. Still I would not move. My obstinate position took some effort, as it was the opposite of my usual nature. I now sat next to GG and patted her still cuffed hands.

After all the other passengers had cleared the gate area, we were escorted off the jumbo jet and led into the terminal by two air marshals. Though not the same two now-injured marshals that had been transporting the Italian drug lord King Caesar back to Miami to stand trial.

We entered the glaring florescent lights of the gate area to the flashes of cameras and chaotic shouts of the press; we saw my Dad holding Penny in his arms and frantically trying to get to us. I was so happy to see him. Tears came to my eyes.

A CNN reporter yelled, "We understand this woman was causing problems on this flight before she attacked the air marshals."

"Why was someone unstable allowed to board the flight?" asked another from Fox news. They continued to holler questions.

It was another six hours before the in-flight video cameras had been reviewed, interviews conducted, and GG was released. Our flight to the Magic Kingdom was long gone and would have to be rebooked.

My Dad was now calmed from his initial hysteria to help his mother and at being reunited with me, and we waited nearby with Penny. I was still clutching part of the now battered Duomo and Tower, which Penny was playing with. The police had taken her Barbie as evidence.

During the endless waiting, GG had been sad about the difficult ending of our trip. She was shattered. She said her head felt squeezed, her body ached, and she was full of regrets. She shut her eyes, and a wave of fatigue washed over her. Then as she continued to wait and recall the events, GG grew angry. She puffed up a little.

"It wasn't our fault."

"Dad, she is right, it wasn't our fault, she was trying to protect me. Protect the whole plane."

"Heroes again; is that what you are claiming? Somehow the airline, the police, and the press don't think so." My Dad was pretty frosty, but he loves his Mom, and he didn't say anything really angry.

GG, with tear-streaked makeup, and me with blood splattered-clothes stood tall as we exited the International Airport. Into the fading Miami sunshine we were greeted by a small group of news reporters that had remained. Stirred into action, one shouted, "Care to comment?"

We were all exhausted. My Dad, now carrying Penny on his shoulders and with a protective arm draped across me, quietly replied with a gentle shake of his head, "No. It was just ah, just a—" He looked at me and leaned down and kissed the top of my head. He rose up high and proud and cleared his throat, "Just a ham sandwich misunderstanding."

Paris, France

"Is this thing working? Can you see me over there?" GG was waving as she was trying out the Ichat feature on her computer. The little camera had been staring at her for several years and she simply ignored it, until now. She said she was missing us and decided she needed to learn yet one more thing on this gadget so she could have face-to-face chats. Sitting in her robe already dressed for bed she was anxious to show off her new skills.

"Sure, GG. Can you see me waving back?" I was also in my pajamas, as my day in California, eight hours earlier had just gotten underway.

"Why didn't you use Face-time?" I asked.

"What is that? Something else I need to learn?" GG asked with no enthusiasm at all.

"It 's easy. I will show you."

She groaned. "Never mind that. Can you hear me alright?"

"Yeah, but you are kind of yelling."

"Mom, you don't need to shout, just speak normally," said

my Dad, who was just out of view, and thinking shouting was normal for his Mother.

"Abby, I just wanted to tell you how excited I am about our trip. And to wish you a bon voyage before you catch your plane." Before GG could continue, Penny came into view carrying a stuffed Pluto and started loudly singing the Disney Hot-Dog song. I soon joined in and then with an awkward leap the family dog, Cooper, a large brown Dobie mix, jumped on the chair with us, and we all tumbled to the floor in fits of giggles. Now GG was looking at an empty chair.

"What a bunch of goofballs." Cooper's head popped back in camera view. "Abby, I will see you in Paris. Au revoir," GG signed off with much happy anticipation.

She had decided it would be best if we met in Paris. Usually, I would first fly to Heathrow before we went to the next big city, but GG got it in her head we would get an extra day in Paris if I flew directly from California to De Gaulle airport.

My Dad was initially not at all happy about me going directly to Paris; it took all GG's considerable powers of persuasion to get him to agree. Keeping my Dad happy meant keeping me safe. GG sometimes had problems with that. Remember London and Florence? Things can get out of hand, though she insisted on thinking of these as misunderstandings.

GG was taking the Chunnel train from London to Paris. That is the train that goes under the English Channel. She would meet me in Paris.

As usual, we had a limo waiting. GG once told me she

always got a special car, not for the car, but because there would always be someone to handle the luggage. She wouldn't have so much luggage if she didn't bring so many shoes.

The huge international airports of the world continued to amaze and thrill GG even though she had been travelling them for many decades. She always acted excited to walk through the doors. Airports she told me were like cities, with shops, cafes, beauty parlors, hotels, news agents, medical centers, and police. Today I hoped we would need none of those services. I wanted to get right to the fun of Paris.

My plane landed 15 minutes early. GG told me that happened a lot on long flights east. She was sure there was some weather or engineering paradigm at work, but she said all she really cared about was we would be at our destination sooner and our time together would be longer. It worked in our favor.

In front of me a steady flow of weary travelers passed through the clanking Customs doors. While waiting, GG quickly inventoried the luggage as it passed by, as she still hoped to one day find her missing bag. Following behind me came the usual efficient but weary airline escort with paperwork to sign. GG raised both hands and quickly flagged us over. GG presented her identification and took the clipboard from the escort and with a flourish signed for me. That was it. I was officially hers, so I jumped into her arms.

On the ride to the center of town we gabbed about Wheels and Penny, school, my friends, and all the delights of Paris.

Turning onto the Place Vendome GG glimpsed our hotel, and she was beaming. "This is it. Time to be a princess, because that is how you are going to feel the moment we walk through the doors of the fabulous Ritz Hotel." She sat tall so I did too. Then she reapplied her lipstick and smoothed her skirt. "The Ritz is synonymous with lavish luxuries of the most obvious kind, and making their guests, that's us, feel special is their daily agenda." This place really suited GG, and I hoped me too.

"Ok, if I am the princess, you must be queen," I said in the spirit of our grand entrance.

"Gerard is the manager, and I see him right inside the door." I looked inside. He was a weedy little man, with fair hair and a sharply pointed nose and stood immaculate, dressed in a light grey suit that matched his eyes. He did not immediately give the impression of the towering presence with which GG said he ruled the Ritz Hotel.

Sweeping out from behind the desk, he greeted GG with a kiss near her hand. Then he looked down at me, clicked his heels together, and in a swift bow declared, "Madame, she is an angel!"

"No, I am a princess," I said with glee as I made a shallow curtsey.

"Oh yes, of course you are that as well. Welcome to the Ritz Hotel mademoiselle, now please let me show you to a Royal Suite."

"Madame Gable, your usual suite is undergoing renovations. Sadly, we had unrefined visitors that were not cautious, and much has to be restored."

"Rock stars?" asked GG, but I didn't hear his reply, as my head was spinning as I took in the stunning interior. Even for GG this place was extravagant.

"We have a very lovely suite nearby with an equally lovely view. Here we are now. May I present the Catherine Suite," he said as he pushed open the heavy fancy double doors.

I had to admit it was magnificent. We stepped through the door and sank into the thick cream Persian carpet. The floors and walls were done out in soft blues and ivory colors. With high ceilings, intricate curlie-que trim, and sumptuous fabrics. A massive pink crystal chandelier was twinkling up high like a cherry on top.

"Positively dreamy, GG."

"Bliss," she replied. "If Grandpa Ted would just walk in right now I would be certain I had made it to heaven." I had to agree, this place was really something.

"Madame has very little luggage for this visit?" said a curious Gerard. "I anticipate, as usual you will be spending much time in our wonderful salons?"

"No, not as much as usual; we are here to be tourists. I want to show Paris to Abby and Abby to Paris."

"GG has a birthday coming up, and she is going to let me help her pick out some new earrings."

"Yes, they are always happy when Grand-mere has another birthday," he replied as he departed with a gentle nod and a palm full of euros.

I was glad he left without mentioning the birthday again. No way to make points with GG. However, she did not have time to get grumpy as I was twirling around and flipping my arms and singing, "Yippee, I am in Paris." The room was filled with such joy GG started twirling too and laughing and speaking French. At least we spoke the few words we knew. "Merci, oui, escargot, patisserie!"

"Viva la France!" declared GG with a deep bow. I responded with a curtsey and jumped onto the bed.

I love to order room service, and part of our travel routine usually included me phoning in a breakfast order as soon as I awoke. My Grandmother gives me no guidelines or budget, and I can be creative. Once I ordered ice cream sundaes for breakfast. GG thought it was a great way to start a day, but this morning I had been more traditional. Coffee and hot cocoa, fresh fruit, and croissants had been delivered. GG was still in her nightgown while we were sitting at a small table in front of the French doors leading to the Juliette balcony. It is called that after Romeo and Juliette.

Eager to start our meticulously planned itinerary GG announced, "The first stop will be the Eiffel Tower. It gives one such a feeling of being in Paris. You must have seen a picture of it many times."

"Sure, the tower is everywhere, but didn't I come here with my Mom and Dad when I was 6?" I was certain I had.

"Yes, but I want to show you my Paris, and you have never seen that before." She was beaming with pride. "I think your Dad insisted on staying on the Left Bank in some artsy place." GG seemed a little miffed that I reminded her I had previously visited Paris. I thought I would change the subject. "Ever see the movie Ratatouille? About a French mouse?"

"Doesn't sound like my kind of film. I once wanted Wheels to watch a French film with me, and he said he would rather wear an Easter bonnet and high heels to Home Depot."

"My Dad wears high heels?" I was astonished.

"No, not that I know of, he was just making a point." GG kept talking, but I couldn't get that picture out of my Dad out of my head. Crazy.

"We can even have lunch up on the tower looking out at the city. I have arranged tickets so we don't have to stand in line."

"I don't mind standing in line for good stuff. One time my Dad and I stood in line for two hours waiting to go on Magic Mountain Turbo Two. It was worth the wait. It was so wild I thought my tongue would fly out my nose."

"That is very unpleasant imagery." She puckered her face.

"Too much information?"

"Way too much. Did you say two hours? Your Father has certainly become a more patient man. Once he left me stranded at a shoe store because he said he wouldn't wait more than 20 minutes. And he didn't! To be honest I didn't notice for more than an hour, but what kind of son leaves his Mother?"

One that hates shoe shopping, I thought, though I didn't say so.

"Ok, time for us to get dressed."

GG liked to think of me as her much-loved granddaughter, but also her protégé, soaking up all the nuances of sophistication and elegant living that a child could. However, as usual when it came to sartorial choices, I have ideas of my own.

"GG, I am dressed. These are the clothes I bought with the money you sent me. You said the theme was Paris chic. The lady at Nordies said that meant black and no frills."

"The lady at Nordstrom is probably a student from the university and has no greater knowledge of France than French fries with her Big Mac." GG looked stiff. "You are ten years too young to wear black. You look like some tortured Sicilian widow on the set of the Godfather movie. No, you must change."

"Ah GG, you are not going to like this, but all of the things I brought are black. Didn't you notice from the plane? Black." I glanced down at my outfit.

"Of course I noticed. I thought you were being practical for the long journey." GG sighed and looked at me with frowning eyes, then let out a small snort. "I suppose we can't let that slow us down. Just for today you can wear your Goth attire. GG turned on her heels and headed to the dressing room.

She emerged in a beige linen pantsuit and navy wooden heeled pumps. She had a double row of pearls and pearl earrings. "Well, what do you think?" she asked me with a smile, feeling confident she looked very smart. After all, this was Paris and GG felt it was essential to make an effort, for it seemed to GG that Paris made an effort to look dazzling for us.

"Looking fabulous, Glam-ma." I called her Glam-ma, which is what my Dad calls her, short for glamorous grandmother. I was sincere and truly intended to flatter her.

"Well, thank you for that." GG accepted my good intentions. "Let's go, Paris awaits!"

"Abby, this taxi ride reminds me the traffic in Paris is just as wild as London, but more erratic and rapid, because they had slightly more room to maneuver." I was relieved when we safely arrived at the Eiffel Tower.

What a grand and impressive sight. The gigantic pyramid of beams and bolts dwarfed the teeming tourists in the sprawling plaza below. I stood at the base and looked high. Today the lines were not terribly long, and with our express tickets we were soon up on the first level observation platform.

Just as the elevator doors, opened GG remembered she hated heights. "Aak!" She pushed back against the rear of the elevator. I took her hand and slowly walked her out through the doors while giving her a pep talk. "Keep going, it is so cool out here."

"Wow, GG, look over the side. Everyone down below looks like little ants."

"Yes, ants," said a slightly woozy GG. She nudged me. "Time to move, we have a lot to do today."

Across the street from the Tower plaza and gardens was the Seine River and the Baton-bus river taxis. GG explained this would be perfect transport for our sightseeing and save us from another harrowing cab ride. Good idea, I thought.

The floating taxi service linked a number of the most famous attractions in Paris and would add to the fun of our day. We boarded, and as we took our seats GG looked down at her feet. She said nothing, but my interpretation from her tight face was she was beginning to feel the pinch of her lovely new shoes. She did not make eye contact with me.

I decided to distract her from her feet. "GG, look at me, I want to take your picture. This boat is neat." We relaxed and looked at the city gliding by the boat windows.

"A long time ago I brought your grandmother Dee Ann here, and this was her favorite part of our visit to Paris."

We exited the riverboat at the Notre Dame stop. This impressive church was as always a busy tourist location, but the lines moved quickly and we soon found ourselves climbing to the top of the Cathedral tower.

GG tried to renege on this, but I really wanted to do it and she could not allow me to go alone or to think she was too old. The narrow, fan-shaped stairs, all 200+ of them, were mocking GG's decision to wear her new shoes. But she soldiered on and up. It was a very slow final 100 steps. At the top we stopped to rest and enjoy the view, though GG's exhaustion kept her from appreciating the panorama. She was eyeing the bench like it was a bed, and I thought she was going to lie down. I went to the ledge and looked out while she rested.

"We must get some postcards before we return to the hotel." She cleared her throat, and her voice sounded raspy.
"Sure, but I don't think there is anything like that up here."

"No, but this is a good time to make a list."

"How many do you think we will need?" She wheezed. GG was stalling for time before we had to begin the journey back to the ground, so I started naming names. Then we started our very slow decent.

"Amen, back on terra firma." GG staggered into the church narthex. I thought she was going to kiss the floor, she seemed so happy to be back on the ground. Then leading the way on inside she took her place in one of the pews. With a limp wave of her hand she encouraged me to look around at the lovely art. I think she was still tired from the stairs. The place was enormous.

After GG got back her breath, which took another full twenty minutes, I begin to get restless. I was now seated next to her, swinging my feet. It was time to continue.

GG slowly stood up from the wooden bench, and I could tell by her face she wanted to howl. She let out a slight gasp and looked at me. "My legs feel like giant redwoods. Sweetie, let's just take it slowly". GG forced a smile and looked at me. Pace yourself, Glam-ma, I thought, this is only our first day.

Then as always, when visiting churches, GG took a few moments to light a candle for Grandpa Ted. A small sign said in French and English "Candles One Euro." GG fished in her handbag for some euros and took an E20 Euro note and folded it. She shoved it through the slot in the coin box. Seeing her do this I said, "You must know a lot of dead people."

"Another hike up those stairs and you can add me to the list," she chuckled. "I just thought some people might not have any change so I should put in a bit extra for them." GG often told me she felt she had so much for which to be grateful.

"You sure do like churches, GG. We have visited a lot of them in different places."

"Yes I do," said GG. "They are places of such glorious ambition with their size, decoration, and good intentions. Look around you." She used her arm to direct my attention. "Churches are full of art and beauty and music and a lot of people trying to be good. However, this is a cathedral, and that means it is even more important to the city and the Parisians. Now we better go; my feet cannot take much more."

"Maybe next time you should light a candle for your feet," I said as I took GG's hand. She pulled me to her and gave me a quick cuddle.

"It would take a blazing candelabra to help my howling dogs today."

The next morning after a good night's rest I was happily bouncing around the suite and jabbering on about the delights of Paris, but GG was not really listening.

Standing dressed in her plush hotel robe in the gold and marble bathroom with its swan fixtures and monogrammed towels, GG was enjoying her elaborate morning grooming. Then she made an entrance. "Oh, let's not talk about Paris; let's head out and enjoy it." I looked down at her feet. She wasn't wearing flat shoes, but they were not very tall — highly unusual.

The remainder of our day was taken up with a trip forty-five minutes outside the city to the Palace of Versailles.

GG really didn't like to drive, and it was universally agreed she was not good at it. Therefore, in light of my Dad's relentless finger wagging on this issue, GG had designed our trip, where possible, to leave others to pilot us along.

The car and driver she had hired dropped us right at the Palace Gate.

The palace and grounds were not crowded today and, of course, were very beautiful. The vast magnificently designed gardens, which surrounded the palace, were in spring dress, with great slashes of colors in precisely arranged patterns and a heady perfume. The place was enormous.

GG told me this had been the Palace of King Louis XIV to which I replied, "There are two Charlies in my class, but only one Louis."

"Not far from here is a lovely village on a big lake with shops and cafes where we can have lunch."

"Works for me, my tummy is empty, but what about our car?"

"I wasn't sure how long we would be, so I asked the company to have a driver pick us up at the lake at 4:30 to take us back to the Ritz. My feet need a break. Let's get a taxi over there," GG said as she pointed to a short row of cars.

I looked down at her feet, but didn't say anything. We had done a lot of walking, and mine were getting a bit tired too.

"Hum? The village is usually a busy tourist location," said GG when the taxi dropped us off.

"Doesn't look too busy to me."

"No it doesn't. That is our good fortune. No waiting." There were five or six cafes along the water all with anxious hosts at the ready.

"What about over there, GG, where it says Fresh Fish?"

"All of these places probably say fresh fish, but they have done so in French. So that place was clever to also write it in English. I think we should reward them and take a look."

On taking a second look, GG was not so certain and seemed to pause. "Hum?" She tilted her head and seemed to be evaluating the amenities. "It's not busy, and sometimes that means the place is not very good."

"Maybe it is not crowded because it is not very fancy," I offered. GG nodded then nudged me forward where we entered the shaded area on the water and asked for a table.

A stumpy, energetic little man greeted us in English. "Welcome. I am Pierre, the owner." He showed us to a wobbly tin table at the water's edge and abruptly bent forward and took a small wooden wedge from his pocket and shoved it firmly under the stuttering leg.

The small metal table was clean and adorned with a fake plastic shell and paper napkins. The general décor left a lot to be desired, and I was surprised that GG wanted to stay.

"Honey, I hope this choice was not a mistake?"

"They seem nice, and the view of the lake is pretty." The owner returned. I smiled at him, then politely ordered a glass of lemonade. GG asked for menus.

"No menus. Fresh fish," said the owner.

"What kind of fish?" I asked.

"Fresh," replied the little man.

GG and I looked at each other, and with a giggle I said, "We will have the fresh fish, please."

At this the man began shouting in French and waving his arms about. A young man and a boy ran out of the kitchen area and onto a small dock. They then untied a small wooden boat and began to push it out onto the lake. Soon the two anglers were positioned about 100 feet off shore and brought out fishing poles and nets.

I looked at GG. "Fresh," she said

"Real fresh."

As GG and I were watching this reality show, I said, "I like to fish too. Maybe I can join them?"

"Sorry, sweetie, I think that boat is not large enough for all four of us, and I could not let you go alone." That made sense, but I bet she would not go even if the boat were big. I smiled at her.

The fish did not seem to be biting and I was getting a

bit fidgety, legs swinging and head bobbing. GG didn't seem to mind; for her it was a relief to be sitting down with her shoes off under the table, looking out at the shimmering lake.

I was almost finished with my beverage and picked up a piece of French bread from a basket that had been placed on our table. "GG, I guess this is why it was not crowded." She nodded in agreement.

"Here, sweetie, write some of these postcards we got at the palace. We can mail them at the Ritz." I took a stack from her and reached for our tote bag. After digging out a pen I went to work.

I had finished three when GG nudged me. "Look." We could see the rodmen waving and holding up two very fresh fish. They quickly began to paddle toward shore.

As they came onto the dock, I took photos of the fisherman with their catch. The fish were quickly cleaned and placed right on an open grill. It was the best lunch GG and I could remember in a very long time. "Well worth the wait," said GG.

I summed it up with a big "yum."

"Perfect timing," said GG as we exited the café area and onto the promenade. "Help me look for a driver with a sign that says Gable." Forty minutes passed.

"GG, are you sure this is the spot?" I looked both ways down the walk.

"Yes, I told them by the cafes on the water. Keep looking."

Finally I sat down on a bench under a big tree. Putting my

elbows on my knees I slowly lowered my chin into my cupped palms. Feet twitching. Neither of us spoke for some time. GG absently smoothed her suit as if being tidy and well prepared would somehow make the driver appear, but of course it did not. GG finally accepted that no one was coming.

With the lovely feel of the lunch long gone, I knew GG was busy putting our options through her mental vegomatic. I was not entirely confident I would agree with her plan, but knew she would have one soon.

With a loud sigh hoping to demonstrate she had struggled with this, "We have two choices, Abby. We contact the limo company and see if they have anyone nearby who can take us to Paris or we just walk over to the car rental place I see down that side street and get a car and get on our way. What say you?"

"We might as well just get a car. That sounds faster. My Dad would understand this is kind of an emergency and not be too mad if you drive us. Just drive careful, ok?"

"Careful, of course," assured GG while thinking of all the places she never wanted to drive were the twisty back roads on the outskirts of Paris. "That's my girl; hop up. Flexibility R-Us."

GG was not usually very flexible at all and was quite annoyed when her plans were derailed, but she seemed to be ok this time. Walking down the narrow street dimmed by the overhanging trees, I was watching GG shuffle along and thought her fabulous pink low heels were not nearly as reasonable as I had hoped they would be.

The small rental agency was located in the shadows of a tall building with a sloping roof that robbed the area of the fading sunlight. We stopped walking in front of a red brick double storefront with the blinds closed. The interior lights appeared to be off, and I fretted they might already be closed for the day.

Just then, a slightly scruffy young man with a mop of untidy hair and a cocky grin emerged from the office, closing the door behind.

"Oh, excuse me. I hope you are not closing. We are desperate for a car. Our limo did not show up, and we need to get to the Ritz."

"Can you please help?" I pleaded.

"I am the generous type," GG said with a big smile.

"She really is too," I offered, hoping double-teaming him would work.

"No, lady I am … well wait, sure," he said as he gazed hawkishly at us, as though he was, on second thought, happy to extend his workday to serve us. "You can have that car right there." He jangled a set of keys in the air. "But I already shut down the office and the computer, so it will have to be cash." We nodded in agreement.

"It is fifty euros, is that ok?" said the young man smiling back. GG nodded again. "Now you two just get in," he said with a sly smile as he held the front passenger door for us.

What a nice young man, GG thought. "Don't you want to see my license or something?" GG asked as she pulled her ID from her wallet.

"Sure, but you look old enough to drive."

Oh no, I thought, GG is not going to like it if he asks her age. But he never did.

Instead he said, "I will just take a photo of your driver's license with my phone and enter your details tomorrow when we reopen." He pulled out his phone and snapped her ID.

"Oh, sorry, but we don't have a parking agreement with the Ritz. Just leave the car on the street nearby. We will just check it on the GPS and pick it up there."

"That sounds easy enough," said GG as she paid an additional 20 euros for this service and tipped the young man 30 euros for making it all so easy.

After the arrangements were taken care of, and GG spent a few moments familiarizing herself with the buttons and gadgets, we were soon waving goodbye. "Look for a petrol station on the left; that's our signal to turn left onto Highway N12." GG accidentally honked the horn and said, "Oops. Sorry."

The trip was meant to be about an hour, but the road was twisty. This in combination with GG's driving skills, and this route was never to be recommended. GG took her time as the road snaked and weaved. Then we hit the main highway, and there was a sudden surge of speed as a zillion cars flew by us.

"We sure could use Wheels to drive us on this road," I said nervously. GG nodded, but did not answer. She just stared intently through the front window. I was holding tightly to the armrest of the door. I looked at GG and decided I should be very quiet. We did make it before it was totally dark, which was essential, as GG's driving went from bad to positively dangerous when the lights went out.

GG gave a yawn and an awkward stretch. She was reluctant to get up from her bed. "Oh, don't turn that light on just yet." She shifted slightly and punched her pillow, then created a small space in the fluffy duvet. I took that as my signal to join her, as she pulled me in for a warm cuddle.

"After yesterday's long ordeal I am feeling a bit of tourist burn out. How about you?" she asked.

I replied with a groggy nod. She then suggested we should do a bit of shopping. Normally, I think shopping is boring, and GG would have to talk me into it, but today I kind of liked the idea of shopping in Paris, and when I told GG this put her in a very good mood.

"Our first stop will be the Vendome Jewel Salon, one of my favorites." GG's eyes were twinkling with joyful anticipation. "Though there are many stores to choose from, it is there we shall choose my new pair of earrings."

I also like jewelry and usually have on a little necklace or bracelet. GG likes to think I got that fondness from her. Maybe I did?

GG told me she always dresses up to go shopping. With a smart style she would feel young and pretty, which gave her the confidence to make very large purchases. I had never noticed her hesitating in that department, but I didn't say so. It was a happy ritual, and today she hoped to make a new happy memory with me.

"Dress up a bit today," GG directed.

"Ok, but it will have to be black."

"No problem at all, we will stop and get you a few things too. But me first!" a cheerful GG declared as she reached in her luggage and brought out a vibrant designer scarf, which she fluffed in the air and tied gracefully around my shoulders. "Voila!"

Entering the Vendome Salon was magical. At least it seemed that way for GG. I thought she was in a trance. "Positively sumptuous," she said as she took a slow turn around. "Abby, this is Marcel the manager." I gave a courteous nod. He nodded in reply, then quickly turned back to GG.

"Bon jour, Madame, we have missed you, do come in." He then greeted GG with a kiss on each cheek. I was glad he didn't kiss me.

"I trust the Ritz is taking good care of you. May I offer you a refreshing beverage?"

"Perhaps later, Marcel, right now I want to take a look around."

"Of course, as you wish." He bowed slightly and brought his arm around in a gesture of welcome.

"It certainly looks like you are staying busy; no recession here," laughed GG. They sounded like old friends. "Abby, keep your eyes open for something special. Diamonds or rubies will do." Marcel was smiling. I started looking in the cases, but to me it all looked like what GG already had.

There were several other people looking in the glass cases at the dizzying array of enormous diamonds and colored gemstones. At the end of the display was a dour woman with a very large grey poodle at her side. It was an amusing sight as the woman also had grey curly hair and wore a long coat of curly grey sheepskin. It was rather difficult to tell where one left off and the other began.

I wanted to point them out to GG. "Psst," I hissed softly. GG turned to lean over to ask me what I was on about, when in a single second the large dog bumped GG and her big diamond earring slipped from her left lobe. In one snap the dog had swallowed it.

GG bolted upright. "Hey you mutt, give that back! Curly, your flea bag just ate my earring!" she bellowed in a most unladylike voice to the curly-coated woman, who then turned to GG with fiery eyes and sniffed, "Cochin!"

That is pig in French and not at all nice. I gave her a mean look, and then grabbed the dog's tail. He yipped, and then turned to look at me and I let go quickly. He was pretty big and did not look at all friendly as he bared his teeth.

The woman had been handling some jewels as this kafuffle unfolded. Marcel looked horrified. He had been standing nearby and rushed over to calm everyone when the grey woman demanded in French, "Marcel please, I need a calming glass of water, sil vous plait."

Marcel turned quickly to retrieve the beverage. As he departed to the back room, the woman and her dog dashed right out the front door.

GG shouted out and headed after her, pushing past the confused security guards, who were astonished that two clients of such a prestigious salon should be in a catfight.

On the street far ahead of us we could see the fleeing woman and her dog. "Hurry it along, Abby, we mustn't lose them." However, GG holding on to me with one hand and with her overstuffed oversized Prada bag in the other and her new red shoes pinching her feet with each step, we were not making much progress in closing the gap.

"You want me to catch her, GG, I am on the track team?"

"Oh no, sweetie, we cannot be separated. I will just try to

go a bit faster." GG was huffing and puffing, but not much faster.

I thought we were about to give up when out of the corner of my eye I spotted the grey woman and her grey dog being seated at the center of the terrace of a bustling Bistro.

"There, GG. She is over there." I was pointing to the woman. GG stopped abruptly and pulled me to the side. GG's gaze did a quick inventory of our options. Leaning sideways against a dirty stone wall and breathless she whispered, "Yep, that's her. How do you like that?" GG fumed as she raised her arm to confirm my spotting. We gazed across to a small center table where Curly was reading a menu. "Look at her, she is going to have something to eat and does not mind at all that Fifi there just had my diamond earring for lunch." GG pulled me back from the corner and continued to keep Curly discreetly in view. "We need a plan."

GG also needed to rest a moment and said so. "This trip is causing a great deal more physical exercise than I'm used to. First the stairway to heaven and now the Paris marathon." That made me laugh.

"Guess we didn't know we should train for the Paris Olympics," I replied.

"I have an idea, Abby."

She always does, so I asked her, "What's up?"

"We will watch for her to leave the table. All of these cafes have the restrooms either upstairs or downstairs and do not use valuable ground-level footage for facilities. The toilets are too small to take that huge hound along, so she will probably leave him at the table. That is when we will snag him."

"How do we know she is going to use the bathroom?"

"She stopped for something to drink. If she is really thirsty we might get lucky?"

"Are we going to get something to drink too? I am kind of thirsty?"

"Sorry. Not just yet; we need to stand guard." We continued to wait. GG had started looking at her watch, which seemed to be slowing down time. Finally, after the woman had downed her second coffee and a glass of water, I was assured GG's supposition was correct. "She can't hold out much longer, GG, that is a lot of liquid."

"So true." Just then the woman stood up and looked around. The plan was working perfectly.

I sat down on a ledge near the wall where GG was leaning, but as soon as the woman whom we now called Curly departed her table I stood up and GG said, "Up, let's go." I was already up, so she must have been talking to herself.

We then casually moved down the street to the edge of the terrace. GG patted my shoulder. "Stay put, sweetie." Then GG gave a furtive look around and carefully after counting to ten to give Curly time to get to the ascending or descending stairway pushed forward to the table, grabbed the dog's lead, and confidently marched away. I followed close behind, walking tall and slowly so not to attract attention.

Several people looked up from their coffee, but no one bothered to stop us or even say a single word.

Once clear of the café and with Fifi leading the way we darted around the corner and into a taxi waiting at a nearby stand.

"Where are we going, GG?"

"Good question." GG leaned back in her seat. "I think we must not return to the Ritz just yet. That horrible woman may have heard Marcel mention our hotel."

"Hotel St Ramon on the Rue St. Germaine please, driver," directed GG. And the small, smelly Renault lurched away from the curb.

"Where are we going, GG?" I again asked in a small, tight voice, slightly worried that we had stolen the woman's dog.

"Oh, to a lovely little hotel on the left bank. It is just a small hotel where no one will bother us." I wondered who would bother us.

"I am certain you will like it. They have a grotto and funny, uneven floors." When we pulled up front I remembered it was the one that I had stayed in on my visit with my parents a few years ago.

Checking into the hotel was easy. It was small and friendly. There were not many rooms or many guests, it seemed. The receptionist, a tiny woman in a severe black, suit broke the austere spell by smiling broadly as she was more than pleased when GG asked for their largest suite.

"The Napoleon suite has a king bed and the Josephine has two twin beds, but is not quite as large. Which would you prefer?" the young clerk asked.

"We will take the larger one," said GG.

I quickly spoke up in protest, "Can we get the one with two beds, GG? You snore."

Startled, GG protested, "I do not and even if I do it is appalling manners to mention it."

"Sorry about appalling, but you do. Snore that is. I even had to put the pillow over my head."

"You snore too" snapped GG "I too will be just as happy to have two beds," she fumed. GG knew that wasn't true.

"There will be a small extra charge for the dog," said the clerk as she nodded toward Fifi, who was now getting comfortable on a rug near the reception window. "Do you have any luggage we can help you with?" she then asked curiously.

We had all but forgotten the dog. "Oh, the airlines lost our bags."

"It happened in Florence too, didn't it, GG?" I was nodding, hoping to enhance our cover story.

"Oh, Fifi just loves to stay in hotels; the doggie fee is no problem."

We trudged up a narrow wooden flight of stairs to an overstuffed room heavy with velvet fabrics and far too many small chairs, which GG asked the porter to remove thinking the big dog was going to need some space.

After the porter departed with a smile and a generous tip I asked, "What are we going to do now, GG?" I knew she was making it up as we went, but did hope to get a general idea of what her scheme was this time.

"We have to wait until Fifi has to go poo, and then we will get my earring back and give back the dog." A simple plan, she explained.

"Eewww. That sounds kind of disgusting."

"I agree completely. So we must hurry things along."

"And just how are we going to do that?"

"I am not sure. I wonder how often they go? I certainly don't plan to wait for Mother Nature."

Our old dog Tanna use to throw up when she ate grass. Maybe we could feed Fifi some grass."

"No. What we need to do is go to a pet store. I have a plan."

I did not know what my grandmother was up to, but a trip to a pet store sounded like fun.

After a half hour to freshen up and rest her feet, we left the small hotel, leaving Fifi in the care of the well-compensated bellman. He promised to supply a bowl of water and a bone from the kitchen. And follow GG's strict instructions not to let Fifi leave our room for any reason.

We headed for the Quai de la Megisserie on the Seine River. It was near the Cathedral we had visited a few days before and in the heart of the city, where GG knew were located a large number of pet stores.

There were pet stores selling from the exotic to the mundane. Loads of shops, I thought, the smells emanating from the busy animal district were gross.

After a bit of comparison, we chose as the most likely store one with a window full of puppies. This display pleased me, but GG wanted to get in and out of there as quickly as possible.

A skinny French guy with spotted skin and greasy hair was attempting to help us, but was totally baffled with GG's request. From her gyrations and pointing to her stomach he seemed to think she was asking about a dog that was expecting puppies. Finally an English-speaking customer came to our rescue with the translation of her request for a gentle laxative for a big dog. Soon we successfully made our purchase and were on our way. This all seemed complicated.

Making our way back to our hotel, GG made a few wrong twists and turns and soon found us standing in an unknown part of town. "Where are we, GG?"

"Not sure where we are exactly." The neighborhood was a mix of apartments and shops. We were standing in front of a costume store. Just then I was thinking we could really use one of GG's maps, but did not mention it because I did not want to offer any encouragement of my grandmother's apparent map addiction.

GG was looking for a cab to make a hasty escape when something in the shop window caught her eye. Corroded metal bars and years of grime obscuring those of us who hoped to peep in guarded the small window. On display in the window were several costumes; one was a fancy ball gown with long white gloves.

"This place looks safe, though slightly grubby, but those gloves are just what we need to get my earring back." GG pointed to the mannequin. Then she grabbed my hand and guided me inside. As we entered the seedy store a tall, very slender leather-clad man in an impossibly tall Abraham Lincoln hat approached. He began to speak in French, then switched to English as GG shook her head.

I need two pair of those opera gloves in the window. Size small if you have them," said GG, pleased he understood English.

"One size fits all. Let me get them for you."

"While we waited I looked around. There were loads of costumes: a mime, a maid, a nurse, and even a pilgrim. The man returned from the back and handed GG the gloves. GG paid cash for the overpriced gloves, and we quickly exited the store.

Still holding my hand and swiftly guiding me to the sidewalk GG said, "I need you to help me look for a taxi." GG was walking swiftly and pushing me down the street. Then soon after a short, twisty ride we were at our backup hotel.

Once in the St Ramon, we looked for the bellman, but were told he was on his meal break and would return in one hour. We went to our room and found Fifi asleep on one of the beds. The sight of the fluffy grey pooch snoring softly among the bedding assured GG she had done the right thing. "See, he is just fine." The dog was clearly not traumatized by the events of the afternoon.

Nearby on a small rug in front of the faux fireplace was a neat pile of doggie poo. "Ah, perhaps Curly too has already thought of a pre-emptive K-9 laxative." The whole thing seemed disgusting, but GG had a plan.

"Look, Abby, we don't have to use the medicine and we don't have to wait."

"Oh, goodie" I said a bit sarcastically as I viewed the poo.

For the first time that wretched morning, things seemed to be turning for the better. Soon we would have the earring and be back at the Ritz. "Time to put the gloves on. First, let's take our clothes off so we don't get them messed up."

Retrieving the earring was not a task that either of us wanted to do, but it had to be done, to finish this whole nasty business.

We wiggled out of our clothes and put on the

bathrobes provided by the hotel. The robes were rather flimsy and a bit rough, nothing like the ones at the Ritz, but we were happy to have them.

Like two surgeons preparing for a delicate procedure we slipped on the gloves. Mine were far too large, but I did not mind. The whole thing just seemed silly. Giggling, we took tissues from the bathroom and GG separated the firm excrement into several portions, and we picked up one half in our gloved hands and while holding our breath squeezed gingerly. We looked at each other with scrunched faces and promptly collapsed with laughter. I made a pretend gagging motion.

"Careful, we don't want to make a mess, though I suppose it is too late for caution now."

I nodded. "Guess this is not something we want to take a picture of to remember about our fancy trip to Paris," I said with a snort.

"You would be right about that," groaned GG with a shake of her head. "I don't want to remember this even ten minutes from now."

"I found it!" I shouted.

"I found it! GG declared.

"Huh?" said GG and we both looked in our hands, and there was GG's earring and also another earring and a diamond bracelet. Or at least GG thought it was diamond, but would not know for certain until the items had been washed.

"GG, what does a diamond become when it is placed in water?"

GG stopped and looked at me with serious eyes. "I don't know, what?"

"Wet."

"Groan, is this another of your riddles? You got me this time."

In the bathroom we cleaned the jewelry with the small bottles of shampoo provided and gave them an extra rinse in the complimentary mouthwash. Just to be safe, GG spritzed them with perfume from her handbag, all while Fifi continued to snooze.

"What we have here, Abby, is a jewel heist that we interrupted. We have foiled a crime. We need to tell Marcel at once." But GG noticed it was late now, and the salon would be closed.

"The jewelry store is closed, so we will go to the police."

"I wonder if Fifi is empty? Maybe there is more in there? Ick."

"True. Perhaps we should give her a bit more time." We stayed in our small suite and ordered room service for dinner and watched some French television. I sat on my bed with my elbows placed on my crossed legs as we were having fun with the sound off making up our own dialogue for the actors.

Fifi had awakened when the food arrived and after accepting half of a Croque Monsieur sandwich for dinner, Fifi went back to the rug she had first used and deposited again.

This was very unpleasant, but had to be done. This time only GG handled the elimination and again found jewels: another earring and a small diamond brooch of a dolphin set with a large round emerald eye.

"I think Fifi is empty now, Abby. Tomorrow is Sunday, and

the jewelry store will not open again until Monday."

"GG, why is Sunday the strongest day?" GG looked up at me suspiciously.

"I give. Why?"

"Because it isn't a weekday." She rolled her eyes, but made no comment. "Honey, I think we will have to go to the police in the morning."

Not again I thought. Now it was my turn to roll my eyes. Soon we were all in our beds asleep, GG and Fifi both snoring softly.

Mid morning the room service waiter delivered a large basket of heavenly French pastry and a cafetiere of coffee for GG and an enormous mug of hot chocolate with whipped cream for me. Fifi was content with two almond croissants and a sausage.

On the room service cart was an English-language newspaper. The headline was impossible not to notice. JEWEL ROBBERY. 2 WOMEN, CHILD, and POODLE HUNTED.

This shocking bit of news shattered GG's assumptions. She had been planning to go to the Municipale Police as a hero that had discovered a jeweler robbery, and now it seemed instead we were being hunted.

"This changes everything," GG said in a panic as she placed her hand on the newspaper.

I was confused. "Is that us they are talking about?"

"I'm afraid so, sweetie, but don't worry, this is just a misunderstanding." GG wished she could talk to Marcel; he would certainly understand what had happened.

Calling it a misunderstanding was not a comfort to me. I had been through quite a few of those with GG, but this seemed a bit more serious.

Unsure what exactly to do, GG worried about how to explain what all had happened in the last 22 hours, but she was certain she wanted nothing to be "lost in translation." And what if the international press got hold of this story?

"Abby, we cannot continue to let Fifi use this Oriental rug as a litter box. Come on, let's take her for a walk. Maybe in the fresh air we can come up with a good idea for how to get out of this."

"Mess," I added.

"No, not mess, a misunderstanding," hastily replied GG.

"Oh yeah, I forgot, a misunderstanding," I corrected, but I was getting slightly worried.

Before leaving the hotel with Fifi, GG locked the jewels in the room safe. And because she did not have a charger, she left her cell phone in the room as well.

GG kept looking in all directions as we left the hotel and headed for a green patch near the Seine to begin retraining Fifi. Which did not take long — apparently, regularity was not an issue for this breed.

We returned Fifi to the bellman. Not wanting to miss another day of Paris, GG took me to the Louvre. "Abby, no trip to Paris would be complete without a chance to gaze at the small, serene portrait of Mona by Leonardo." She also said the next few days might leave little if any time for trivial tourist pursuits until we straightened out the dog thief.

After seeing the Mona Lisa, Winged Victory, and the Venus de Milo, which GG called the tourist trinity of the Louvre, we had a huge lunch in the museum's finest café.

As lunch was finishing, GG explained to me what was going to happen next. "We have to go to the police now, and it will be boring and maybe a bit scary, but please don't worry."

"Not like it's the first time for us in a police station," I said with a shrug. We finished at the museum and went to turn ourselves in.

The police station for this Arrondissement, or area, of Paris was in a large, old building and was still busy with the miscreants and victims of the previous night. It was a bit daunting.

GG and I waited in a long, gloomy crocodile of ominous looking Frenchmen and tourists. When our turn finally arrived, GG told them we were there to report a crime, a jewelry theft. We were rewarded with a litany of disinterest. The moody clerk thought we had been mugged, so dismissed us as he used his pen to point us to yet another line and then went back to his paperwork.

GG didn't move. "No, we have not been robbed, we have stolen jewelry, no that is not right. We have in our possession stolen jewelry, well, not actually on us, but we know where it is," blathered GG. The man whose desk had a sign which read he understood English did not seem interested in hearing the fantasy ramblings of a middle-aged woman and a kid, especially Americans, and did not even bother to again look up.

GG was clearly frustrated and knew in these situations you could not just let yourself be trampled on, or worse ignored, but having no energy to protest in French she said to me, "I think we need some new clothes and someone other than the Sunday crew here to help us. Let's go on with our sightseeing and try this again later."

We finished our day with a trip to the hills of Montmartre. This GG told me had always been the artistic heart of Paris, but today it seemed almost sinister as we kept a keen eye out for anyone that was putting a keen eye on us.

The domed Church of Sacre Coeur sits majestically on the summit of the hill of Montmartre. This is the highest point in the city, and the view of Paris from the stairs that sprawl below is pretty amazing. However, this day GG felt no desire to explore the interior of the gleaming basilica or linger at the view. GG's enthusiasm for touring was pretty low, and it showed.

We went instead to the Square at the top of the Palace du Tertre. There were exotic and eccentric inhabitants, all trying to make a buck off the tourists. Street artists producing portraits and caricatures of tourists caught my attention. "GG, can I get one of these pictures?"

"That's an excellent idea. I would love that." GG needed to rest her nerves and her feet and gratefully rested her derrière on the rough surface of a low stone wall. The young artist swiftly started making chalk lines and I was excited to see what he was doing, but he told me to remain still."

"You look much like the people from the newspaper. I don't suppose you are car thieves?" he chuckled as he continued to sketch.

GG and I exchanged quick looks. "Car thieves?" I said.

"What!" said GG "What picture? I didn't see any picture."

"Oh please, Madame, I am an artist, I see people differently perhaps. But you and your little girl look much like the photo in Le Monde, but I know this is a little jest."

Le Monde was the largest daily paper in Paris. In French, naturally, so GG had not bothered to look at it to see if there was additional information about the jewelry theft. But what did he mean about a car thief?

GG was now quite alarmed and I was confused. "Abby, we need to get back to the hotel. Right now!" She stood abruptly and as if the grotesque little bronze gargoyle on the parapet had taken a bite, she tore a gash in her skirt. Turning quickly to survey the damage, with her large handbag she knocked over the artist's can of turpentine filled with a selection of used brushes. As she jumped unsuccessfully to avoid the splashing liquid she broke the heel on her shoe. Then as if in slow motion GG leaned against the barricade and sank slowly down the wall, where she plopped to a halt on the stone walkway.

The artist and I stared in amazement. GG stared at her feet. She was a mess.

I did not feel like laughing. I felt sorry for her and knew my grandmother hated mess and dirt of any kind, and she was covered in it. GG always carried wet wipes and hand sanitizer and even often wore gloves so she did not have to touch the filthy banisters and doorknobs of a grubby big city. So immediately I dove into her handbag. "Wet wipes, GG?" I held out a packet. I wanted to make her feel better.

"No, honey, I would need a whole box and a fire hose for this disaster," but she smiled at my question and attempt to comfort her. GG then waved aside the artist's offered hand as she struggled to her feet.

"Is my picture finished?" I asked, worried and thinking we needed to get going.

"Yes, just enough."

"Let's go," GG said as she scrambled to tidy herself and grabbing my hand.

"Madame, you have forgotten your portrait," said the artist, who had already been paid for his work and was busily rolling the paper.

GG grabbed the portrait and together we stumbled toward the waiting queue of taxis.

"Are we going back to the police? I asked, hoping we did not have to do that again.

"No, we are going back to the hotel and hope no one there saw our photo," GG whispered to Abby, hoping the driver did not understand English.

As we neared the hotel, our hopes for a discreet entry were dashed when we saw two police cars out front. "Stop, stop," GG shouted to the driver.

We gasped as we gazed through the smeared taxi windshield and saw Fifi taking a Poodle-perp-walk to a nearby van. In silence we looked wide-eyed at each other.

We needed a plan and quick. Nothing much came to mind, except I knew GG needed to get out of her torn, smelly, flammable clothes.

GG, knowing now we were hunted, felt certain we could not be seen at her usual shopping boutiques. When all was said and done, there was only one place left to shop with anonymity. She quickly gave the driver new instructions and looked at me with apology in her eyes. I replied with a small, tight smile.

As the taxi approached the now familiar Costume Boutique I said, "Here please."

"You really do have a good sense of direction; I thought we were nowhere near." She paid the driver and we got out and stood gazing into the barred windows.

"Ah, here we are again," I said as we pushed through the door.

"Oh it is Opera Gloves and the Merry Widow. I thought you might return. So often people come here to find the right costume to relive their youth," smugly teased the tall man that had served us on our previous visit and who was now extravagantly dressed as a cowboy.

"Well, Tex, my youth seems some time ago right about now, but yes I do need a few things." GG told him her list.

"No need to be sensitive here, cheri," he said. "I'm sure I have just what you need. In your size may I suggest the nun or the nurse? Oh, or perhaps the witch?"

Emerging from a curtained corner that functioned as a fitting room, GG glanced in the mirror and I did a double take. I couldn't help it; I started to laugh. GG responded with a deep-throated very loud laugh, but it wasn't joyful laughter.

GG stood there wearing a long black skirt, a spider web woven top and black platform cage shoes, which she said felt surprisingly comfortable. Except for missing a tall pointy hat she looked just like a storybook witch.

GG was always dressed pretty, but standing in this shabby shop in these garish clothes, you could tell by the look on her face she felt all had been lost. However, my grandmother is made of pretty tough stuff when necessary, and this was no time for tears.

"I will take them. And did you happen to get Le Monde today?" she asked casually. "I need to find a copy."

"Yes I did, and may I say tisk tisk, it is a shame how the camera adds ten pounds." GG and I went stiff and looked at each other.

"What! You know?" she exclaimed.

"I keep everyone's secrets, darling, it is part of the job, usually a very lucrative part of the job," he said with a sly wink.

GG paid up, for the items and the discretion, then he handed her the newspaper and a bag with her damaged garments. GG just shook her head. "Just the paper, toss away the clothes, but don't put them near a flame or they will go boom," GG cackled loudly as we left the store.

Outside the shop GG opened the paper. There we were on page two. American Crime Spree. I turned to my grandmother, and my mouth dropped open. I slowly closed my mouth and said nothing. GG looked at me and exhaled slowly as if to say there is nothing left to say.

GG felt certain she could turn our situation around if given the chance to speak directly to Marcel before going to the police again. That was not possible until the morning, when the jewelry salon reopened. She was not sure what was going on with the car thief story, but we needed to get our hands on an English-language paper. "Abby, keep your eyes open for a news stand so we can find out what is going on."

"Why not check the Internet?" I said.

"You're an angel. Give me a hug." Which I did at once, as I really needed a cuddle about then. "Of course, that is what we will do. Let's go to the train station; there are plenty of Internet cafes around there. Abby, don't make eye contact with anyone. Keep your eyes on your feet." We walked away, eyes down, and I was wondering what my Dad would say if he knew what was going on.

We found a café off the beaten path, and GG quickly went online and read all about us. Gulp. This was not good news.

Headline: Americans on Crime Spree. First there was the story about being hunted jewel thieves, which we already knew. Then there was a story that a Parisian gang robbed a rental car agency in a small lakeside town and stole seven cars. They had drugged and kidnapped two employees and put them in the trunk of a car later found parked on the street three blocks from the Ritz hotel. According to fingerprints, CCTV photos, a photo of a driver's license found on the phone of one of the men arrested, the police had concluded the American woman traveling with a young girl was the getaway driver.

We finished reading. We were stunned silent. Finally, I gave a shiver. "Were they really in the trunk?"

"I am afraid so." GG had a sad look on her face

"I hope they are ok." Softly I asked, "What now?"

I could see GG's mind was whirling. I was sure she had a plan, but all she offered was a shrug of unknowing.

Whoa, that was scary. GG always has a plan. "Come on, we need to find a place to hang out until tomorrow when Marcel is back at work."

"Do you mean hide out?" I asked.

GG looked at me, still sad faced and nodded yes. Then she took two big breaths and stood up. She seemed revived. "A plan?" I asked.

"Yep. Follow me. Let's take a short cut through the train station."

As we were walking through a maze of travelers and mounds of luggage, I abruptly stopped. "GG, I think that is your bag over there. The one from Florence."

GG turned in the direction I was pointing and eyed the designer bag with the extra strap that was on the ground at the feet of two rough looking men. There were loads of people walking by in every direction.

GG seemed to forget we were hunted criminals and headed directly to the men. When the bag was at her feet she leaned over for inspection. She was not at all discreet. I was right behind her, but looking at the men from the corner of my eye.

"Hey, Grandma, back off," said a big, smelly guy. I thought he was scary, so I tugged at GG's skirt, thinking maybe she did not hear him. She did.

She rose up abruptly and with astonishing boldness said, "Grandma says you are a thief, young man, but you should know I stole a car on Friday and some jewelry on Saturday." She was on a roll. "You look pretty small time to me." He looked puzzled.

"Yeah, and we kidnapped two people and stole a big dog too," I jumped in. GG and I gave each other a quick head jerk.

"Wooo wooo, you two sound real dangerous." He taunted us and glared, then snickered to his mate.

"This is my bag, and I want it back."

"No chance, Granny," said the other man standing there as he gave us a fierce look, meant to intimidate. It worked on me, but apparently not GG. She leaned over and pulled on the handle. The big man shoved her, but she did not let go. Then he looked like he was going to hit her so I kicked him in the shin, which probably didn't hurt him, but did get his attention. Things were very intense and several people nearby started moving away.

The mean guy picked up the bag and jerked it from GG's hands, but he stumbled back and dropped it. The bag plopped right down on the concrete, and as it did the bag bounced, then fell open. Out clanked a dozen pieces of beautiful sterling silver, packets of money, and a gold box. A swag bag.

We stood back, astonished and horrified. Seconds later, a policeman who had been alerted to the scuffle was heading our way, blowing a whistle. The men took off running toward the station so GG grabbed me, spun me in the direction of the street, and yelled, "Run, Abby, run!" I did and took off as fast as I could, without looking back. I didn't stop until I turned the corner. The policeman had chosen to chase the men and the bag, so we were free.

I was breathing heavily, and GG was making loud gasping sounds.

"Abby, darling, we need to sit down. Which direction was that Internet café?" I pointed, and we headed off at a much-reduced pace.

Inside the small, grotty café we sat. There was no table service, but GG gave me some money and I went to the counter and got two cold Pepsis. My heart was still pounding.

When I returned with our sodas GG said, "Well, at last we

know what happened to my bag. Stolen by a couple of creeps." I wasn't sure if that was her bag, but it didn't really matter. I was just relieved we hadn't been arrested. And hoped that if it was her bag, her name on the tag was not still on it. We sure had a lot of explaining to do, and so far no one to listen.

GG was an avid reader of crime fiction, and told me we could not use her credit card for a hotel, and any nice hotel would take more cash than she had. If she went to an ATM, CCTV could track us. Instead, we went to an all-night cinema and bought tickets for the next three films.

"This is kind of fun, GG, I have never spent the night at the movie theater."

"You are a great kid. Let's hope it is fun. They are showing The Sound of Music in French, Russian, and Spanish.

We loaded up on snacks and entered the dark theater. GG found a short, empty row in the very back and we settled in. She was tucking her purse between us, then said, "If anyone tries to steal this bag we might as well let them. I think I only have a few euros left."

The theatre was mostly empty. Down toward the front were some people, but it was too dark to see much.

GG tore up Kleenex and stuffed the little wads into my ears. "Are these R-rated or something, GG?"

"Not at all, but the music is rather bold, and we don't want it to keep us awake." We quickly ate our junk food and curled up in each other's arms. We were fast asleep before the first opening credits had finished.

We awoke at about 5 a.m., when a lumpish attendant was clanking the doors and trash cans. I felt icky.

I pushed myself up from the seat with a groan. I was stiff

and sore. "That was quite a night. How ya doing, sweetie?" She ruffled my hair that I am sure was pretty messy already.

I replied with a groggy nod.

We exited the cinema after a brief stop in the basement ladies' room. It appeared clean, but the wallpaper was peeling and the stench of disinfectant sucked the air out of the cramped room. The low ceiling was very oppressive. "Abby, what a way to start a day in Paris."

"What a way to start a day anywhere," I replied. Spending the night in a movie house was not as fun as I had hoped. GG shuddered.

Eight low-wattage bulbs surrounded the bathroom mirror in a failed attempt to evoke Hollywood, but only three still glowed. GG stared into it. "We look homeless, Abby."

"We sort of are, at least right now." In the gloomy light I could see that GG's eyes were hollow and darkly rimmed from lack of restful sleep. I was glad the mirror was not more well lit, as it would probably make my grandmother feel bad at what she might actually see.

We fussed about washing our faces with soap from the dispensers, and as the eco friendly art house had air dryers instead of towels GG brought out tissues from her handbag which we used to pat our faces dry.

The purse also provided us toothbrushes, as GG never left home without hers. Luckily she had a spare for me.

"Any chance of some floss in there? My braces are a mess." I asked as I pointed to her big purse. She shook her head no.

Sadly, one look at our hair though and I knew there was nothing in her handbag that would make a difference.

We inspected each other. I made a face curling my lips.

"I don't feel much like a princess anymore. I need a bath." GG agreed our efforts were not a big improvement in our general hygiene or appearance, but it had given GG a few minutes, while spraying both of us with perfume, to collect her thoughts and prepare to execute Plan B, or was it Plan C?

GG refused to let our ghastly appearance or our hunted status get us down. "Heads high, big smile, off we go."

GG's shame at her current couture faded as she gathered her wits and prepared to claim the glory we had earned for thwarting the jewelry heist. And she hoped also to explain what had happened at the rental car agency. "Abby, the events of the last days might seem to have eroded our natural optimism, but we will need it back. In the meantime we will fake it."

"Sure," I said, with little conviction.

I looked terrible, but felt remarkably casual in accepting all the twists and turns which had blighted our Parisian stay. I really liked Paris and was glad I was having a chance to visit, but I was anxious to get all of these misunderstanding sorted out.

Still blinking awake in the pearly morning light that greeted our exit, Paris now appeared grimy and grey. As we made our way from the theatre the weather seemed to be plotting against us, as a heavy morning mist was adding to our already bedraggled appearance.

At this hour there were few people up and out; street sweepers, delivery vans, and impatient people walking impatient dogs. In the quiet was the thunk, thunk of GG's cheap shoes that seemed to mock us as we went down the sidewalk.

With several hours before the Jewel Salon was to open, we stopped for breakfast at a hole in the wall café just out of sight of the main boulevard.

The coffee machine hissed hello as we entered the tiny eatery. GG told me we were in no hurry so to order whatever I wanted. I approached the counter and carefully studied the cloth-lined trays of pastries. I picked three. That made GG smile. "Starving, kiddo?" I nodded yes.

While waiting for our food I was squirming in my chair and moving my jaw side to side in contemplation. "Do you think they will believe us, GG?"

"Oh yes, we just need to talk to Marcel and make sure he told the police how nice we are."

"What about the car? How do we prove we didn't steal that car?" Things had gotten quite out of our hands pretty quickly, and I was not sure even GG could get control back. GG liked control.

"That one is kind of tricky. They do seem to have a lot of evidence that we were involved. My plan is to ask them to fingerprint the money from that guy's pocket. It will prove we paid for the car."

"Sure, that might work." I was not really convinced. Our food was delivered to our small table. Nice surprise, the food in the poky little place was tasty and a much-needed pick-up. It was, however, served by a surly old man.

Normally GG would have been surly right back, but she did not have the energy that day, so she made a friendly gesture toward the grump in hope of softening our future service, and I gave him a big smile, which was not returned.

GG spent a great deal of time stirring her coffee, first one direction then the other, splashing a small amount on the scarred wooden table, then sopping it up with the waxy serviettes. We had a lot of time to kill. I too was unusually inanimate.

Time was dawdling. "GG, did I tell you Nathan broke his toe in a Karate competition and still took second place? By the time he got home his toe was all purple and gigantic." GG was so inert she just looked up and then back to coffee stirring.

"We have a new family next door. Hunter and Isabelle. She is in Mrs. Robinson's class." I took a bite and another swig of cocoa. "They moved from Seattle. Their Mom said if she stayed there much longer she was going to rust." GG was still gazing at her cup. I went back to lazily dunking each of my choices in my milky cocoa. I ate all three and even the remains of one GG left unfinished. If we sat there much longer I would have probably eaten three more. It was something to do.

Empty time seemed to make it drag even more so I continued to attempt conversation, but my heart wasn't in it. "GG, I know a secret; want to hear it?"

She looked up at me. "Sure, kiddo, spill." She knew what I was doing, and smiled. "Better yet, I know a secret; want to hear it?"

"Oh yes, please." I perked up.

GG looked over at me and slightly raised her eyebrows. Softly she said, "Gladys Gail." She shook her head slightly and added, "That's me."

I looked at her with a slight grimace and a quick wave of revulsion. "Gladys Gail. GG?"

"Yep, my two grandmothers. Gladys and Gail."

"Don't you worry; that secret is safe with me. Promise."

"I just thought you deserved to know."

"GG, it is!" I got up out of my chair and went over and threw my arms around her neck and gave her a big hug. I thought she needed one. She sat up and seemed revived.

"Ok now, let's hope the caffeine and sugar rush soon jolts us into action. We have a busy day ahead."

GG looked at her watch. There was nothing left now but to face the police. GG anticipated a tiresome day and felt it only fair to prepare me for what was ahead. She really did not know how to, so she simply pulled me closer into her arms for another warm embrace and kissed the top of my head.

We cleared our small bistro table and tossed the trash in a wicker basket near the counter. At precisely ten o'clock, GG handed the grump twenty euros and asked to use the phone. I was surprised when he agreed.

GG called the Vendome Jewelry and spoke to Marcel. She told him what had happened and where he could find the jewels. However, Marcel assured her the jewelry had been discovered and returned to them when the dog had been picked up. Marcel said GG's own earring and phone were with the police and gave her the name of the officer and location we needed.

Then we caught a taxi with the last of our cash. We prepared for our interrogation as we bumped along in the back seat. "Don't be frightened, sweetie, it is me they are mad at."

"GG, you didn't do anything wrong, and I am going to tell them."

"Thank you, but I think it will probably be best if you don't say anything at all. Now here we are."

Getting out of the taxi we both looked up, as we were shocked to hear a familiar voice.

"Mother! Abby!" shouted Dad as he emerged from a curbside bench. "Oh, at last I have found you." Having regained our composure after the sudden sight of my Dad, GG said calmly, "I am so happy to see you, son." I ran to my Dad's arms.

"We have had such a lovely time. Paris, you know, is one of my favorite places." GG was amazingly chirpy while ignoring the way she was dressed or the reason for being found at the police station. Or even my Dad's presence at all. I was dumfounded, but so happy to see him.

"Mother, you can stop? And please no tourist dialogue, I have seen the papers and the Interpol memo; that is why I am here." My Dad then reared back in surprise, and he reached up and took off his dark glasses and his big blue eyes smiled out as if seeing his Mother for the first time. "You do know you are dressed like a witch?"

"It is Paris chic," we sang out in unison as we dissolved into uncontrolled laughter, which caused us to shake and snort, and GG's eyes became teary. My Dad couldn't help himself; he chuckled too.

"You two are nuts. Ok, Mom, let's get this sorted out," and inside we all went. GG was grateful for my Dad's appearance, no matter how inconvenient his line of questioning. She was worn-out and happy to have him help with the police.

The next several hours with the police were exhausting mounds of paperwork and relentless questioning. I mostly waited in the hall with my Dad. The police had already apprehended Curly, a known jewelry thief and had worked to find a new home for Fifi.

The young car thugs had been insulted when the police had believed GG the mastermind, and they totally denied she had any involvement, so all charges were dropped in the car theft and kidnapping matter.

We were exhausted, but relieved when at last we were allowed to depart, as the police were satisfied with our story and the recovered jewels. I felt like running to the exit doors of the Police Station.

We were back curbside, and I was telling my Dad about the good things we had done in Paris when GG said, "Did you say Interpol? Well, that is a new one even for me."

"Yes, Miles Kingford, my grad school roommate, is with the State Department now, and he saw the memo and sent me a notice. He also sent the French police a letter of reference on your behalf.

"As you know, I was at your Fisher Island place for the Miami design conference, so I went directly to the airport and took the first flight here. I have been looking for you for 24 hours."

GG was nodding her head. We were waiting for a car and our luggage, which had been sent by the Ritz. I didn't really care if any of the luggage made it. I felt like I had been in the same outfit for a month, and I was too tired to much care. GG had also asked for the hotel's assistance to get my flight confirmed, and herself on the next Eurostar to London.

Sitting there, I hugged my grandmother. "I love you so much, GG. We always have the best holidays. Where are we going next time?"

"You really want to go with me again after all this?" GG surprised herself with a sudden burst of self-pity as her eyes became teary. "It certainly would make me very happy." I took a tissue from her bag and handed it to her. As she blotted her eyes, she looked at my face and quickly began to perk up. "I guess we did get to see a lot of Paris." Her energy surged. GG was not one to accumulate regrets. She once told me they took up too much mental closet space better used for happy memories, but she would very much regret doing anything that would cause an end to our Grand Tour.

"I shall begin researching the perfect destination as soon as I return to London." GG sat tall. "I have a couple places in mind already."

My Dad quietly said, "Of course you do," but didn't say anything else. I think he knew his Mom couldn't take much more today, but he was not joining in our plans for future trips.

I turned to my Dad to seal the deal. "Dad, you and Mom would not want me to miss out on all that neat culture, and there are loads more cities we need to check out. Yeah, and we have been to at least 100 churches. That has to be good for a kid, right? All that other stuff was just misunderstandings."

GG was beaming, and we gave each other a big cuddle.

Soon the Ritz limo pulled up, and while the driver held the door we all three shuffled inside.

"To De Gaulle Airport," said my Dad. "I texted Miles, and

he got me on the same plane as you, Cupcake." He hugged me close.

"I am going back to London for a long bath, a new hairdo, and a toxic bonfire made of witches' garb." GG shook her head with disgust as she slightly raised the hem of her black skirt and eyed her attire for her trip back to London. She then chuckled and shook her head in acceptance. I guess she was too tired to much care. I know I was.

When we had our luggage on the curb at the airport loading and unloading zone, and hugs were given all around, GG climbed back into the big car to continue to the Eurostar terminal.

A back window of the limousine glided down, and GG leaned toward us and waved. "Au revoir," I said while waving back and blowing kisses.

GG smiled really big and said, "Be sure and pick up the dog at oversized baggage claim."

As the big black car pulled away from us my Dad shouted, "Wait! Stop!" He was waving his arms frantically and cried, "What dog?"

The End

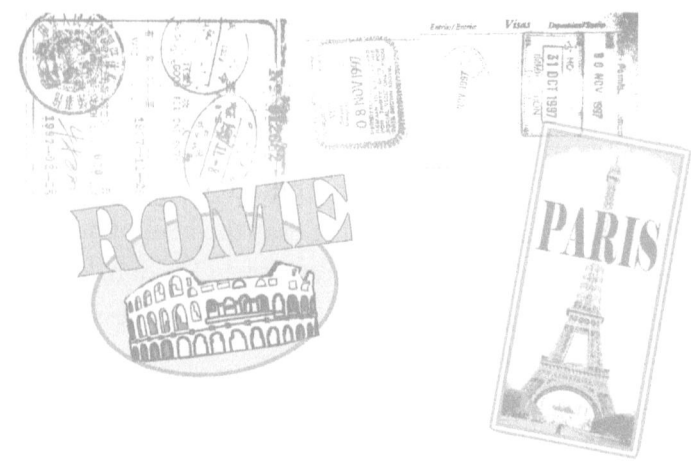

*Abby and I hope you have enjoyed
our fictitious adventures.
We have certainly enjoyed sharing them with you.
Bon voyage.*

Helpful Information

Annie Oakley — Famous wild west sharpshooter

Boho Chic — (Abbr). for Bohemian Chic (flower power)

brogues — style of shoe

Calamity Jane — Famous American frontierswoman

cassock — floor length priest robe

Dollywood — Country themed amusement park

(The) DL — The Down Low - something kept discreet

DNA — individual genetic information

fruition — completion

gherkin — small pickle

Hee Haw — Country themed television show

LAX — Los Angeles International Airport

Leonardo Da Vinci's "Vitruvian Man" — Leonardo was a great Renaissance artist who created a now-famous architectural drawing of the proportions of a human man

Miss Marple — A crime sleuth character created by Agatha Christie, the best-selling fiction author of all time.

Nancy Drew — A girl sleuth created by Carolyn Keene, a pseudonym used by several authors.

Orient Express — Elegant long-distance train that runs through Europe and Western Asia

PG Wodehouse — Author of British class satire

paradigm — relationship of ideas or outcomes

posh — well off, high class

Romeo and Juliette — Characters created by William Shakespeare

salon — elegant shop or store

Scotland Yard — Main police headquarters in London

solidarity — harmony, shared aims

swag — plunder, stolen items

vegomatic — blender

Vespa — Classy Italian motor scooter

TRANSLATIONS

ITALIAN to ENGLISH

Benvenuto a Firenze	*Welcome to Florence*
Buon giorno	*Hello, good day*
Ciao	*Hello, goodbye*
Alto	*Stop*
Signora	*Adult woman*
Signorina	*Young girl*
Bellisimo!	*Extra beautiful*
Abigaile	*Abigail*
Andiamo	*We go*
Bella Figura	*Beautiful figure or presentation*
Questura	*Type of Italian police station*
Carabinieri	*Type of Italian law enforcement officer*
Poliza	*Police*
Subito	*Immediately*
Buona notte	*Good night*
Conto rappido	*Check or bill quickly*
Giovedi	*Thursday*
Per favore	*Please*
Grazie	*Thank you*
Rinascente	*Renaissance a revitalization of art in 1400s*

Il Gazzetino	*Italian language newspaper*
Piazza	*Plaza or public square*
Fame de lupo	*Hungry as a wolf*
Al fresco	*Cool, fresh*
Momento	*Moment*

FRENCH to ENGLISH

Bon Jour	*Good day*
Oui	*Yes*
Au Revoir	*Goodbye*
Bon Voyage	*Good Journey or Voyage*
Madame	*Adult woman*
Mademoiselle	*Young woman*
Ma'am	*Abbr. for Madame*
Viva la France	*Long live France*
Le Monde	*French language newspaper*
Cafetiere	*Coffee-maker*
Arrondissement	*Area, borough*
Gendarme	*CentralePolice station*
Municipale	*Municipal, public*
Coiffeur	*Hairstyle*

BRITISH ENGLISH to AMERICAN ENGLISH

Wonky	*Wacky, not normal, slightly odd*
Trolley	*A cart with wheels*
Flat	*Single story apartment or condo*
Abbey	*Monastery or convent*

About the Author

April Gamble

Just like GG, I am a widow and split my time between Fisher Island, Florida, and London, England. And also like GG, I enjoy traveling the world with my much-adored granddaughters, Abby and Penny. However, unlike the book, I don't like high heels. I don't mind aging, and happily I have had very few misunderstandings.

www.ingramcontent.com/pod-product-compliance
Ingram Content Group UK Ltd.
Pitfield, Milton Keynes, MK11 3LW, UK
UKHW041945230426
12048UKWH00008B/147

9 781614 932505